For Joan, the music and poetry of my life.

With all my love, Jim

*For my daughters Christina and Melina,
the critics and tasters who guided me in the creation of
my garlic recipes, co-author Charlie Fox for his tireless support,
energy and total dedication to spreading the word about
glorious garlic – and last, Marty, my black lab and
other four-legged beasts who shared my life.*

Lynn

For Erik, a son that parents dream about having!

With love, Dad (Charlie Fox)

To Dr. Candi for restoring my faith in physicians Lynn

THE GARLIC CURE

By

James F. Scheer

Lynn Allison

Charlie Fox

THE GARLIC CURE

First Printing, April 2002
Second Printing, May 2002
Third Printing, January 2005

Authors- James F. Scheer, Lynn Allison and Charlie Fox
Publisher - Alpha Omega Press, a division of Alpha Omega, Inc.
Printed by- J&M Companies - www.jmcompanies.com

International Standard Book Number: 1-931916-01-2
Printed in the United States of America

Order ID: 104-6484260-5006665

Thank you for buying from Levis JCC Thrift Shop on Amazon Marketplace.

Shipping Address: Kathy Kennedy 1111 North Street YREKA, CA 96097-2010	Order Date: Shipping Service: Buyer Name: Seller Name:	Mar 12, 2010 Standard Willis M Price Levis JCC Thrift Shop

Quantity	Product Details
1	**The Garlic Cure by Scheer, James F.; Allison, Lynn; Fox, Charlie** **Merchant SKU:** 1008504 **ASIN:** 1931916012 **Listing ID:** 0116G348RY1 **Order-Item ID:** 11270539511042 **Condition:** Used - Very Good **Comments:** Pages crisp and clean with minor wear to the cover; personal inscription on first page.

Thanks for buying on Amazon Marketplace. To provide feedback for the seller please visit www.amazon.com/feedback. To contact the seller, please visit Amazon.com and click on "Your Account" at the top of any page. In Your Account, go to the "Orders" section and click on the link "Leave seller feedback". Select the order or click on the "View Order" button. Click on the "seller profile" under the appropriate product. On the lower right side of the page under "Seller Help", click on "Contact this seller".

Thank you!

Acknowledgments

Our special thanks go to the hundreds of researchers who carried out the garlic studies on which this book is based. We salute these truth-seekers, many of whom worked without grants for the benefit of us all.

Joan Davidson-Scheer created the books's title when the rest of us were at a loss to find the name that properly characterized its subject matter. She also performed web research, verified facts, edited and did the computer formatting. Take a bow, Joan!

Lynn Allison expresses gratitude to her daughters and dozens of friends for sampling the book's recipes through the years and for their constructive recommendations to make something great even greater.

Charlie Fox thanks the millions of individuals on four continents who have heard his garlic lectures and radio broadcasts for the past three decades. Their questions have made him aware of the information most pertinent to their interests and needs - important to determining this book's contents.

Jim Scheer is grateful to Stephen Langer, MD, a collaborater on many of his books, for his helpful suggestions in developing *The Garlic Cure*. He salutes Lee Swanson, a longtime friend, and a constant source of encouragement and inspiration to him through much of his writing career.

No one deserves our gratitude more than Steve Tweed, our brilliant editor.

Our joint thanks go to writers of dozens of testimonial letters relative to coping with human and pet disorders with aged garlic extract and to Wakunaga of America for the company's cooperation in supplying research and historical background information that made writing our book possible.

James F. Scheer
Lynn Allison
Charlie Fox

Foreword

Before they made seemingly endless voyages, seafaring Vikings, who supposedly discovered America centuries before Christopher Columbus, never failed to lay in a rich supply of garlic for the crew.

And they had no history of on-board illness such as that of others who sailed for month after month - the later English, Portuguese and Spanish explorers, the majority of whose crews were stricken with scurvy and its vitamin C deficiency symptoms such as swollen, bleeding, fetid gums, loosened teeth, soreness, anemia, overwhelming fatigue, collapse and death.

Even after 5,000 years, garlic continues to be the favorite folk medicine all over the world - and with good reason; it is effective in preventing and coping with a host of varied diseases.

However, in this age of sophistication, most medical professionals depend almost entirely on prescription drugs and medicines and shrug off garlic and other leading herbal remedies as something from the Dark Ages.

Yet the shrugging-off becomes more difficult due to many well-structured studies showing the efficiency of garlic and the exponential growth of patients' knowledge about nutrients and the embarrassing lack of knowledge in this field of many doctors.

Patients are increasingly frightened by reports in respected medical journals of 100,000 annual deaths caused by allopathic medicines, as well as hundreds of thousands of serious injuries from side effects.

Patients know that few medical colleges teach nutrition and that most doctors are too busy learning about allopathic medicines from drug companies to study nutrition. Therefore, when physicians discount the value of things they know little about -- natural foods and supplements – and claim that they are dangerous, patients tend to lose confidence in them and skim the Yellow Pages for an alternative physician. Surveys show a marked trend of patients away from conventional treatment.

It is time that doctors face up to the evidence that most modern diets are deficient in vitally needed nutrients and that patients would rather take safe preventive measures – natural foods and food supplements – in order to remain or to become non-patients. In the past 25 years, more than 1,300 studies have demonstrated garlic's incredible ability to build superb health and to manage many illnesses.

Modern medicine is based on curing illness. Alternative medicine is based on preventing illness and promoting wellness and longevity. That's what this book is all about.

Everybody concerned with wellness, with his or her physical and mental ability and the energy to set and reach goals with the wellness of the immediate family, relatives and friends should read *The Garlic Cure* and pass on its information. This is truly a superb guide, not only for surviving on this Polluted Planet but for thriving here.

Inasmuch as most of the cutting-edge research cited in this book has been performed with aged garlic extract, this type of supplement is frequently featured in these pages. Sometimes, aged garlic extract is referred to as "aged garlic" for the sake of brevity. However, in every instance, aged garlic means aged garlic extract.

And the gourmet, garlic, health-enhancing recipes created by Lynn Allison bring an added dimension and bonus value to this book. Those I have sampled only serve to entice me into trying all 139 of them.

James F. Scheer, Lynn Allison and Charlie Fox (no relative) are well known for writing and dispensing honest, well-researched and pertinent health information. They've done it for many years. Once you've read *The Garlic Cure*, I know you'll agree with me that this is the most comprehensive, factual and brightly written health book on garlic of all times!

Arnold Fox, MD, physician in internal medicine, cardiology and anti-aging and host of the radio talk show, *The Universal Anti-Aging Network.*

Los Angeles, California

Table of Contents

PLEASE NOTE

The purpose of this book is to provide accurate and authoritative information in regard to subjects covered. It is not intended to offer medical or related professional advice. If you have any medical condition or are taking prescription or non-prescription medications, consult your medical professional before beginning any new conventional or alternative therapy or discontinuing the medication or treatment you are currently receiving.

After I read over 100 scientific reports from medical centers all over the world on the protective and healing aspects of unique aged garlic extract, I started using it in my practice. Just as aged garlic belongs in everyone's natural medicine cabinet, this book belongs on their "must read" list. Inexpensive, exorbitantly safe, well-researched, and useful for a myriad of conditions as well as age-proofing your body, you owe it to yourself to effortlessly become a garlic expert.

Sherry A. Rogers, MD, ABFP, ABEM, FACAAI, FACN author of *No More Heartburn, Pain Free in 6 Weeks,* and the soon to be released, *Detoxify Or Die.*

Introduction

One of the most amusing stories about garlic comes out of a tragic situation in 18th century France.

During the bubonic plague of 1721 in the seaport of Marseilles, city officials decided to use four criminals condemned to death to bury thousands of infected bodies in the streets and, in the process, to die from exposure to them.

Day after day, the criminals carried out their work, remained in good health, and, eventually, went free, because they knew something that Marseilles officials didn't – that crushed garlic mixed with red wine, a folk medicine, supposedly protects against illness. Night after night, they "protected" themselves liberally. There were then no double-blind studies to prove the value of their concoction. However, the criminals didn't need them. They survived, and some of the officials who had condemned them didn't

These days we know quite a lot about raw and aged garlic, but there's much more to know about their awesome preventive and curative powers. So many new studies are coming at us so quickly that it's easy to miss out on vitally important information. What we don't know **can** hurt us. What we do know can help us and those closest to us. The purpose of this book is to offer the latest helpful and little-known information on garlic in relation to a vast range of illnesses.

Almost all of the studies cited in these pages – many of them double-blind from respected labs throughout the world — have been conducted with aged garlic, which the vast majority of authorities concludes is the most effective type of garlic. Only comprehensive epidemiological studies have been included. However, both kinds have been subjected to careful analysis by us to assure their validity.

This book offers a two-fold approach to preventing and treating disease — through aged garlic supplementation and through raw garlic in cooking with "touched by an angel" recipes created, tested and used for decades by gourmet chef Lynn Allison. Once you try them, you will use them for a lifetime!

Welcome to the pages of *The Garlic Cure.*

James F. Scheer
Lynn Allison
Charlie Fox

Chapter 1

Things You Should Know About Garlic

Once upon a time, convincing most doctors that garlic can prevent and cure many diseases was like trying to reassemble a fallen Humpty Dumpty. Even the most glowing research was dismissed as "folk medicine."

However, now, after more than three thousand successful garlic studies – many double-blind – physicians concede that there's more to garlic than meets the eye – or the nose.

The National Cancer Institute's Designer Foods Program, directed by the late Herbert F. Pierson, Ph.D, demonstrated serious governmental effort to discover and isolate healing substances in garlic, linseed, licorice root, citrus fruit and members of the parsley family, to determine what effects they have on human health and to design foods that capitalize on them.

In numerous talks to the media, Dr. Pierson named garlic as the food on which his group was concentrating – the one most promising for preventing cancer and other devastating diseases.

"Garlic is the one we're going after. None of the other foods even comes close," he said.

Findings of Drs. John T. Pinto and Richard S. Rivlin, researchers at the prestigious Memorial Sloan-Kettering Cancer Center, validate his statement. Aged garlic slowed the progression of prostate cancer by means of its unique sulfur compound called by the unspellable name S-allylmercaptocysteine — SAMC, for short. Yet even results of a well-structured study don't convince all doctors. They have to know the "whys".[1]

Here Are The Reasons

Fortunately, the Sloan-Kettering researchers were able to determine these reasons: SAMC decreases the production of certain proteins that cause harm, including prostate-specific antigen (PSA), a promoter of cancer cell growth, and speeds the breakdown of the harmful dihydrotestosterone form of the male hormone testosterone, which initiates cancer in some middle-agers and beyond. Dihydrotestosterone's negative influence was discovered when the spread of prostate cancer was blocked by castration, hardly the treatment of choice for the sexually active.

The product used in the study was Kyolic, aged garlic made by Wakunaga of America, Ltd. Only properly aged garlic will form SAMC. It is not present in other brands of garlic that aren't aged or in fresh garlic. These researchers discovered that slowing prostate cancer growth by as much as 70 percent required 1/4 to 1/2 teaspoon of the aged, liquid garlic extract taken two times daily with meals. They ranked prostate cancer as the second most common cause of cancer-related deaths of American and European males.

A high calorie intake, heavy in animal fat, seems to initiate this kind of cancer, according to many researchers. Prostate cancer is almost non-existent in Thailand, where little animal fat is consumed. In contrast, it runs rampant in Denmark and the Netherlands, where large amounts of animal fat are consumed.[2]

A Disaster Happening

Still other researchers relate high rates of prostate cancer – all types of cancer, for that matter — to eating far too much Omega-6 essential fatty acid (EFA) in widely used safflower, sunflower, peanut, and soy oils – and margarines made from them — in ratio to Omega-3, a lopsided 25 to 30 parts to one. More about the seriousness of this imbalance in contributing to critical physical, emotional and mental disorders later . . .

The Pinto/Rivlin report also indicates that derivatives of sulfur in garlic inhibit the growth of transplanted tumors and apply the biochemical brakes to the spread of breast cancer, melanoma – one of the deadliest malignancies — and neuroblastomas (cancer of nerve cells). (Garlic's successful war against all types of cancer merits an entire chapter. This will come up shortly.)

New studies have sparked an explosion of optimism that garlic may prevent, alleviate or cope with many medical ailments over and above ever-threatening cancer and cardiovascular conditions. Following are the most frequent ailments to enter doctors' offices: colds and flu, Candida albicans (yeast infection) fatigue, and other illnesses caused by environmental poisons and heavy metals intoxication.

With the common cold uncommonly common these days, most people – at the first sneeze – think of vitamins C and A and zinc. Not bad thinking, but it excludes another helpful nutrient: garlic.

The Cold Facts

Anybody who has endured a cold knows that its main symptoms are nasal secretion, a stuffy head, a cough, sputum, a sore and gravelly throat, headache, fatigue and feeling miserable. For sore throats, grandmas used to squeeze juice from a bulb of garlic and mix it with warm water for gargling. For a recurrent sore throat, Andrew Weil, MD, recommends a modern version of grandma's cure: two diced cloves of garlic mixed with food.[3]

Thirty-nine Japanese hospital patients with colds were given Kyolic with vitamins B-1 and B-12 and a liver decomposing extract at a rate of 1 ml per administration in a gelatin capsule twice daily. No other health foods or medicines were permitted.

Patients were asked to grade 15 symptoms of colds according to positive or negative reactions to Kyolic with vitamins B-1 and B-12: Effective (almost all symptoms improved); Slightly Effective (some symptoms improved; and Not Effective (no symptoms improved). The percentage of Effective response or better was 53.8% and Slightly Effective or better at 89.7 %. [4]

It is a generally known fact that antibiotics are helpless against viruses that cause colds and flu. So biochemists writing in the *Japanese Journal of Infectious Diseases* introduced influenza viruses into the nasal passages of mice. Those who received Kyolic aged garlic extract resisted the illness. All of the mice controls came down with the flu. [5]

The powerful influence of garlic on colds is nothing new. More than a half century ago, garlic proved to lessen the severity of symptoms of colds and reduce their duration.

A German physician, Dr. J. Klosa, reported success in treating clogged and runny noses, sore throats, coughs and other miserable symptoms of colds with two grams of garlic oil in a kilogram of water – plus some onion juice – 20 to 25 drops every four hours. This treatment was taken by mouth and also by nostrils.

All 13 cases of grippe (a severe, many symptom cold), fever and catarrh were ended much quicker than by the usual treatment with no lingering after-effect such as lung inflammation, swollen lymph glands, coughs, jaundice and pain in muscles and joints.

Each of 28 cases of sore throat cleared up in 24 hours – more quickly when treated in early stages. Seventy-one individuals with stuffy or runny noses got total relief in 13 to 20 minutes with no complications. [6]

When an influenza epidemic swept across the Soviet Union in 1965, a 500-ton emergency supply of garlic was airlifted in, and government-controlled newspapers in Moscow and other major cities urged the people to eat more garlic, because of its ability to prevent contracting the flu. [7]

The condition of the immune system determines how quickly colds and flu are healed, and the trace mineral selenium in garlic contributes to healthy immunity.

One of the world's foremost authorities on selenium in cancer prevention, Dr. Gerhard Schrauzer, now professor emeritus in biochemistry at the University of California, San Diego, states that the considerable amount of selenium in garlic is important to its healing powers.

"Linked with prevention of cancer and heart disease, selenium stimulates the immune response," he says. "This means that garlic can help to handle allergies and the common cold. A natural antibiotic, it can prevent infectious diseases such as pneumonia, tuberculosis, dysentery and diarrhea." [8]

In recent studies at the University of New Mexico School of Medicine and the Albuquerque Veterans Administration Medical Center, a preparation including Kyolic Aged garlic extract was found to be effective against the influenza B virus and the Herpes simplex virus II. In fact, it was so successful that a patent application has been filed for this formula's use against Herpes simplex II. [9]

Beating Candida Albicans

Almost epidemic these days, Candida albicans, yeast overgrowth, contributes to chronic fatigue, weakened immunity, irritable bowel syndrome and various food intolerances. Its four main causes are increased use of antibiotics — particularly tetracycline — a heavy and regular intake of sugar (the favorite food of Candida albicans), use of the Pill and cortisone.

Many years ago at various medical seminars, biochemist Jeffrey Bland, PhD, advised doctors to decimate the candida with daily intakes of garlic for a month and then recolonize the colon with two to three billion units of acidophilus daily. Over the years, a preventive medical specialist, Stephen Langer, MD, of Berkeley, California, has had success with more than 100 Candida patients with 200 to 400 mg of Kyolic aged garlic capsules daily and the amount of acidophilus recommended by Dr. Bland. Actually garlic and acidophilus don't necessarily need to be taken in sequence, inasmuch as garlic appears to kill harmful bacteria but helps friendly bacteria to thrive, adds Dr. Langer. [10]

A diet rich in sugar – even sugar in fruits such as bananas, prunes, dates, or figs – can diminish the value or possibly undermine the garlic-acidophilus regimen. It can also be harmful to diabetic patients

Preventive medicine specialist Ronald Hoffman, M.D., of New York City, advises his diabetic patients to supplement their diet with garlic, along with an array of vitamins and minerals.

"Diabetics tend to develop yeast infections more, because yeast thrives in a high sugar environment. Garlic suppresses yeast. The deodorized capsules are best," he claims. [11]

Energizing Fatigue

Inasmuch as a patient's fatigue is usually attributed to hypothyroidism (low thyroid function); hypoglycemia (low blood sugar); overwork; prolonged sleeplessness, one of the anemias; mononucleosis, or chronic fatigue syndrome – to name the principle causes — most doctors prescribe or recommend medicines or nutrient supplements specific for these disorders.

One of the anti-fatigue remedies rarely considered is garlic, although a historic precedent for it dates back to ancient Egypt and Rome. Historians tell us that soldiers, sailors, and laborers were rationed garlic to relieve their fatigue and help them to recover quickly from exhaustion.

Egyptian laborers who constructed the Great Pyramid at Giza were issued a daily supply of garlic to renew their energy. During an economic belt-tightening period when the pharaoh cut out the garlic, the laborers staged the world's first sit-down strike. Faced with a "no garlic, no pyramid" ultimatum, the pharaoh gave in.

Roman soldiers frequently massaged their bodies with raw garlic to ward off colds. It also warded off their wives. Athletes in the first Olympic games in Greece ate garlic for strength and endurance. Many of today's athletes do the same.

In two tests of energy and endurance, mice given a supplement of Kyolic (aged garlic) were able to swim 82.3 and 90 percent of an allotted period, as opposed to 50 percent by those who had taken none. On a treadmill, mice taking Kyolic ran for 1611 consecutive seconds, in contrast with controls able to run for only 929 seconds – just about half as long. [12]

Another endurance experiment with mice resulted in even more dramatic results. Five animals given garlic extract for 60 days and five others were compared – actually, contrasted. The unsupplemented mice swam to exhaustion in four hours and 15 minutes. One of the garlic-supplemented mice stopped swimming after nine hours. The other four were still swimming well after 10 hours, when the experiment was halted. [13]

It Stimulates People, Too

A test to discover if aged garlic extract prevents fatigue and enhances recovery from it in human beings was conducted by the Nihon University School of Medicine (Japan). Twenty student members of a college athletic club were subjected to severe physical stress – continuous track and field type exercises and exhausting swimming programs for three hours daily. All 20 students received the same foods and experienced identical training conditions, including the same amount of sleep. However, 10 were given two milliliters of aged garlic extract (AGE) after breakfast and dinner for 22 consecutive grueling days. The 10 others received a look-alike placebo. [14]

Bio-markers showed better prevention of exhaustion and recovery from fatigue in takers of AGE. Complaints of both groups were high, almost identical, about fatigue, pain, stiffness and drowsiness after the first marathon day and decreased slowly through the test. However, the complaint rate was significantly lower in the AGE-taking group on the test's last day.

On the objective side, the AGE group showed a slight increase in blood sugar. Normally, with exercise, the blood sugar declines. Further, the AGE group showed greater grasping and back muscle strength than the control group. Significantly, the patellar reflex, long established as an objective measurement of fatigue, demonstrated marked improvement among AGE-takers. Exactly what is patellar reflex? There's a simple way to know. When the doctor gets you to cross one leg over the other, he gently taps the area just below your kneecap (the patella). The slowness or speed at which your leg swings out is a measure of your fatigue.

Aged garlic also reduced harmful triglycerides, an unexpected dividend. Elevated triglycerides are considered a greater threat of cardiovascular disease than high cholesterol levels. The biochemists who conducted the study wrote "These results suggest that AGE is an effective medicine for the prevention of and recovery from fatigue."

Pollutants Everywhere

Over and above revving up our energy, garlic fiercely protects us against toxins in the environment. Complaining to his doctor about how difficult it is to live in health on this Polluted Planet, a patient remarked —

"There are three actions I can take to keep from being poisoned – stop eating, drinking and breathing."

A less drastic action is taking garlic regularly.

Industrial city smog turns many a blue sky into a hazy, dirty gray. For the first time, studies in the United States, Brazil, Europe, Mexico, South Korea and Taiwan show conclusively that air pollution in the developing world not only harms infants, old people, and the infirm but also unborn babies, causing stillbirths and infant deaths. Results of this research were coordinated and analyzed by Beate Ritz, an epidemiologist at UCLA's Center for Occupational and Environmental Health.

"Air Pollution doesn't just impact asthmatics and old people at the end of life. It can affect people at the beginning of life, and that can disadvantage people throughout their lives," Ritz told the

Los Angeles Times. [15]

Another category of pollutant – on the ground as well as in the air — are insecticides, herbicides and fungicides. Used in farm areas and home gardens, they kill insects, weeds and fungus and, at the same time, do away with yellow clouds of butterflies and chirping birds and are subtly and slowly doing away with us.

Additives extend the shelf lives of processed foods while decreasing the length of our lives. A former rat poison called fluoride, widely used in drinking water, toothpastes and mouthwashes to prevent tooth decay, fails in its main purpose, as shown by solid studies in respected publications, reduces our immune power and makes us vulnerable to many serious diseases.

Aluminum, mercury, lead, cadmium and other all too prevalent environmental toxins commit internal sabotage that exhibits itself in a medical book full of ailments that often defy conventional diagnosis.

A non-nutrient, the mineral aluminum invades us in foods, beverages, medicines, and cosmetics — in processed foods such as baking powder, baking powder biscuits, processed cheese, cheese sauces, pickles, salad dressings, salt and other seasonings (aluminum keeps the latter two free running) white flour, fruit juices and soft drinks in aluminum cans, aluminum foils for wrapping and cooking foods and city water that uses alum to reduce sediment.

Aluminum also assails us in antacids, antidiarrhea formulas, antiperspirants and deodorants, some cosmetics and feminine hygiene products (including douches) some hemorrhoid salves, lipstick, skin creams, lotions and toothpaste. One important theory maintains that aluminum contributes to or causes Alzheimer's disease. This will be explored in the next chapter.

Beware of Mercury And Lead!

Don't overlook mercury from among many environmental and man-caused sources of illness – coal-burning and amalgam fillings of teeth — and in large ocean fish such as shark, marlin and swordfish – that threaten us with kidney failure, tremor, diarrhea, neurotoxic effects, birth and genetic defects, serious mental problems and, occasionally, death.

Some people believe that banning leaded gasoline many years ago means that lead-poisoning is a thing of the past. However, the malady lingers on. This lead didn't disappear by Merlin magic. Still on roadways, it is thrust to roadsides by millions of whirling tires, carried onto farmland and wind-blown into streams and lakes and, then, enters the foods we eat, the water we drink and the air we breathe. Other major lead sources are factory smoke, cigarette smoke, insecticides, some hair-colorings and cosmetics, newsprint and canned foods.

This significant quotation appeared in a *New York Times* article, The Threat of Lead Pollution," on April 16, 1994: "Exposure to lead is considered the most serious pollution problem facing children." Lead poisoning causes nerve damage and brain damage and difficulty in learning, hyperactivity and attention deficit disorder in children. It contributes to high blood pressure in adults and increased chances of cardiovascular complications and death."

Cadmium poisons us in tobacco smoke, in smoke from zinc foundries, water and contaminated soil.

Dramatic Discovery

How heavy metals damage our liver and the rest of us and how garlic protects us was dramatically illustrated by Benjamin Lau, M.D., a professor of microbiology and immunology and an award winning researcher at Loma Linda University Medical School. Dr.

Lau filled ten test tubes with human red blood cells, then added lead to two, mercury to two, aluminum to two and copper to two. Nothing was added to the remaining two test tubes, left as controls. (Copper is a needed trace nutrient in minute amounts, usually no more than three milligrams daily. However, above this amount, it may upset the zinc-copper balance, increase free radical attacks and raise the chances of heart attacks and strokes.)

Then he added aged garlic to one each of the tubes containing the heavy metals. In those without the garlic, the heavy metals ruptured the red blood cells, spilling their contents and annihilating them. In those with added garlic, the heavy metals seemed tamed and harmless, a biochemical testimonial that aged garlic protects red blood cells from heavy metal sabotage. [16]

Dr. Earl Mindell cites a small study that validates the protection of the liver against amalgam (mercury and silver) fillings by aged garlic. A Honolulu dentist used garlic to treat 14 patients with mercury fillings. He found that garlic is actually an oral chelator, helping patients to detoxify their liver by throwing off the mercury. [17]

National and state dental associations continue to declare that amalgam fillings are not harmful. However many studies show otherwise. Not long ago, the California state legislature went on record criticizing the California State Dental Association for not letting patients know that there are non-harmful alternatives to mercury fillings.

Liver: The Inner Protector

Several studies show that a healthy liver uses enzymes such as glutathione S-transferase and superoxide dismutase (SOD) to detoxify poisonous chemicals, converting them to harmless water-soluble compounds that drain away in the urine. Like other organs, the liver has limitations. Constant abuse causes faster use of transforming enzymes than they can be synthesized. Then the undermined liver collects fat and eventually develops sclerosis (hardening) that can become fatal, as in extreme alcoholism.

So prevention through avoidance of toxins is the best first measure. Next comes taking aged garlic daily to strengthen the liver itself and its function, assuring enough transferase enzymes, and antioxidants to protect liver cells from free radical damage.

One of the most convincing studies proving that Kyolic Aged Garlic Extract guards the liver from even devastatingly toxic chemicals was reported in the *Hiroshima Journal of Medical Science.* Human liver cells in a tissue culture were doused with carbon tetrachloride, a chemical noted for causing liver cancer. Garlic guarded them against damage.

Fights Carbon Tetrachloride

A study in the *Japanese Journal of Pharmacology* explains that carbon tetrachloride causes triglycerides (fats) to invade liver tissue, making the victim prone to develop liver hardening and disability or cancer. Given carbon tetrachloride, mice sustained liver damage and then were fed aged garlic that blocked the liver from forming new fat.

In his youth, one of the writers of this book, Charlie Fox, worked for several years in the factory production of floor wax containing carbon tetrachloride and was diagnosed with fatty liver, a threat to his survival. His health suffered through the years. Then, by regular outdoor exercise, eliminating processed foods, including sugar, eating more fresh vegetables and fruit and whole grains and taking 400 mg or more of aged liquid garlic extract twice daily, he was able to reverse the condition.

Fortunately, use of carbon tetrachloride in industry and the dry cleaning business has now been banned. However, old supplies of this chemical still exist in some homes and offices.

Ionizing radiation bombards us daily from many sources – not only x-rays and devices for treating tumors – but common appliances: microwave ovens, radios, TV, electric blankets, and even electric or telephone wires. In a study of lymphocytes, human white blood cells of the immune system, in a culture of living tissue, some samples were infused with raw garlic, others with L-cysteine and the third with Kyolic Aged Garlic Extract. A fourth was not protected with garlic. All samples were exposed to 2000 rads of radiation.

Lymphocytes in unprotected tissue died within seconds. Most of them infused with raw garlic extract lasted for three hours. However, every lymphocyte died within 24 hours. Eighty percent of the lymphocytes infused with aged garlic or L-cysteine were alive and well at the end of the 72-hour experiment, causing the researchers to conclude that aged garlic and L-cysteine guard against radiation damage and are powerful antioxidants. [18]

Blocking The Aflatoxin Threat

Beyond coping with radiation and toxic chemicals, aged garlic appears to prevent aflatoxin poisoning produced by a fungus called Aspergillus flavus, which changes the character of human liver cells on the way to making them cancerous, as shown by biochemists at Loma Linda University. Of the 16-plus toxic compounds secreted by this fungus, aflatoxin B-1 is the most deadly, causing mutations in a host of microorganisms, as well as in animal and human cells.[19]

Peanuts, other nuts, rice, grains, corn, beans and sweet potatoes are sometimes contaminated with Aspergillus flavus, generally caused by excessive rainfall in the growing season or storage in a damp place. This fungus was discovered about a generation ago when 100,000 turkeys in the British Isles suddenly died. Government animal husbandry investigators found that the turkeys had been fed moldy peanut meal and that the aflatoxin had killed them. Subsequent testing demonstrated that aflatoxin is a powerful cause of liver cancer in animals. [20]

Interpretation of various studies by authorities differs as to whether or not aflatoxin is toxic to human beings. However, the

Loma Linda study indicates that an increasing incidence of human liver cancer in Africa and Asia has been related to the intake of aflatoxin in areas where agricultural and food technology remain in a primitive state. Growers and processors of peanuts operate under a voluntary self-policing rule of monitoring product for mold, testing samples for aflatoxin, and discarding affected product. However, small amounts of aflatoxin have been found in peanut butter by *Consumer Reports.*

So it's buyer beware. When you eat nuts – any kind — it's always a good idea to check them carefully and discard those that are moldy, discolored or shriveled. If the taste of a nut is sour or bitter or different in any way from the usual, spit it out right away. If by accident, you ingest suspect nuts, Dr. Langer suggests taking a 200 milligram capsule of aged garlic as a neutralizer.

Aflatoxin occurs in peanuts, despite the best efforts by growers and processors to prevent it. However, a whole group of chemicals in foods that stress the liver are put there on purpose. We know them as additives – preservatives, emulsifiers, artificial sweeteners, fragrances and coloring agents, to name the major ones. Although the Food & Drug Administration assures us that they are safe and necessary and that the gains from them outweigh the risks, it is impossible not to be skeptical – and with reason.

The Fallacy of Single Tests

Many of the estimated 11,000 additives have been tested individually and declared safe. However, there's no way to assure that they're not harmful to lethal when taken with other additives. It would be physically and financially impossible to test all their interactions to one another.

A statement made by the prestigious English medical journal *Lancet* sums up the situation in a few words:

"The question of the ultimate effect of food additives on man is still unanswered." [21]

P. R. Peacock, past Director of Research at the Glasgow (Scotland) Royal Cancer Hospital, expresses skepticism from another standpoint:

"With synthetic substances that have never existed before, the tissues and cells of the body have no previous experience." [22]

A prominent authority who would rather remain anonymous voices his objections in this manner:

"The five pounds of food additives taken in each year by people who eat processed foods may undermine more than their own health. They sabotage the health and vitality of future generations. The threat from these chemicals may harm us in many ways, but they will do even more silent sabotage to our children. And how can our children even begin to trace their illnesses to specific causes?"

The Good With The Bad

In any event, food additives add more substances alien to the body for the liver to neutralize by means of detoxifying enzymes that make them more water soluble for elimination through the kidneys and the bladder. However, enzyme reactions don't come without a cost. The cost is cell-damaging free radicals, which can cause cirrhosis of the liver. The more additives taken in, the more difficult the liver's job and the more reason to support it, first, by subtracting as many additives as possible through minimizing or eliminating processed foods and, then, by giving the liver adequate nutritional support.

For more than a quarter century, animal studies have shown that aged garlic extract supplementing the diet counteracted the toxic effects of many artificial food colors – FD&C Red No. 2, FD&C Blue No. 1 and FD&C Violet, among them.

When these dyes were mixed into the animals' regular food – at 5 percent of total diet – they developed diarrhea – the body's way of ridding itself of toxins – stopped normal growth and failed to groom themselves. Aged garlic taken with the additives returned the animals to normal function. [23]

Information in this chapter just begins to offer the little-known health benefits of raw and aged garlic. There's much more coming up about ailments they help to prevent or mitigate – allergies and arthritis to devastating conditions such as AIDS and Alzheimer's disease.

Chapter 2

Dealing with Allergies, Arthritis, Alzheimer's and AIDS

After his alternative doctor suggested that he take a 200 milligram capsule of aged, deodorized garlic three times daily as part of his health maintenance program, a patient asked a broad-based question:

"Even though garlic is well-known for preventing cardiovascular diseases and cancer, what can it do for me?"

"A better question is what **can't** it do?" the doctor replied and showed him the book that listed 26 ailments that garlic helps to prevent or mitigate. "And that's not the end. Almost every week, there's a new study that reveals garlic's influence on still another disorder."

Actually, aged garlic has some influence on an entire alphabet of ailments, as demonstrated by anecdotal evidence, clinical research, double-blind studies and much of the biochemical investigation reported in this book.

A Alzheimer's disease
B Breast cancer
C Candida albiçans
D Diabetes, Type II
E Ear infections
F Fever and fungus

G Gout
H Heart disease
I Ileitis
J Jaundice
K Kidney ailments
L Leprosy and Lupus
M Meningitis
N Neuritis
O Otis Media
P Pneumonia
Q Queasiness
R Rheumatism, rhinitis
S Sinusitis
T Typhoid fever
U Urinary ailments
V Vaginitis
W Worms
Y Yeast infections
Z Zits

A Weapon for the Taking

New research indicates that garlic may be able to help the four A's – allergies, arthritis, Alzheimer's disease and AIDS.

One of the toughest problems with allergies is discovering which foods or environmental pollutants deliver the allergens that cause the sneezes, wheezes, bronchial spasms, runny noses, watery eyes, itching skin, headaches, sinus congestion, depression and — according to certain authorities — weight gain and even some types of arthritis.

Unfortunately, such symptoms don't conveniently appear right after the intake of or the exposure to an allergen. Some come as much as 24 hours later. Best bets for discovering food allergens are Rinkel's Rotary Diversified Diet and the Coca Test.

Here's the Rinkel procedure. Eat just a single suspected food at a meal and then refrain from eating it for four days. Then try it. If you're allergic to it, you'll experience a flare-up. If you're not, you'll be symptom-free. Test all suspected foods by this procedure.

The Coca Test works like this. You start before getting out of bed. Find your pulse on the inside of the wrist. Count your pulse for 6 seconds and multiply the beats by 10 to obtain a resting pulse rate. Then eat a suspected food and repeat the test. Test yourself again 30 and 60 minutes later. If your pulse rate increases 20 or more beats from the resting rate, you're probably allergic to that food and should skip it.

Allergy Prevention

There's general agreement that allergy-prone people produce an over-abundance of complex proteins called antibodies. These trigger specialized cells: mast cells – in the skin, intestines, lungs, stomach and throat — and basophils – located mainly in the blood vessels — to release histamines. Histamines cause tiny blood vessels to enlarge and become more permeable, allowing blood to leak into surrounding tissues, causing local inflammation.

To prevent allergic reactions, histamines must either be neutralized or blocked from being released. Vitamin C is perhaps the best vitamin for neutralizing or blocking histamines. Stephen Langer, M.D, a preventive medical specialist of Berkeley, California, finds that 1,000 milligrams three times daily work best for this purpose. Quercetin, too, helps nullify histamines – 500 milligrams twice daily — and slows or stops the production of substances that cause inflammation. [1]

Histamine-caused symptoms differ in different parts of the body – hives in the skin, congestion and inflammation in nasal passages, tears in eyes, and contraction of smooth muscles in the walls of the lungs, blood vessels, stomach, intestines and bladder.

Certain nutrients taken daily enhance skin and mucus membrane integrity and the maturing of immune system cells. Most professionals suggest 8,000 International units of vitamin A, 50 milligrams of vitamin B-complex to strengthen immune function and 1000 mg of vitamin C three times daily to boost lymphocyte and macrophage activity, to raise levels of interferon, scavenge free radicals, fight viruses and strengthen connective tissue, increasing resistance to allergens and vitamin E — at least 400 IU – to quench free radicals along with vitamins A and C.

Biochemist Richard Passwater, PhD, a world authority on pycnogenol and writer of several best sellers on this subject, tells us that "the first recommendation of most European physicians for hay fever and related allergies is the versatile anti-oxidant-bioflavonoid pycnogenol." [2]

Warfare in a Test Tube

Three studies by Dr. E. Kyo and associates, of the Pharmacology & Safety Assessment Section, Institute for OTC Research in Japan, show that aged garlic is also valuable in coping with allergies.

In the first, the biochemists staged test tube warfare between an allergen and two different opponents — an anti-allergy drug and aged garlic extract (AGE) on the battleground of immune system cells. To make the problem more difficult, they added a chemical that always causes the release of histamines. AGE blocked histamine release more effectively than the anti-allergy drug with none of the side effects of that drug.

In the second experiment, a well-known skin irritant (picryl chloride) was applied to the ear of a human being, followed by the intravenous injection of an antibody that induces skin inflammation. Taken orally, AGE showed its histamine-suppressing ability by reducing the swelling by between 25 and 45%.

When AGE and the anti-allergy drug were fed into the stomach, after the application of picryl chloride to the ear, AGE's effectiveness topped that of the drug 24 hours later.

In the third experiment, picryl chloride was applied to belly skin of a human being. Seven days later, it was applied to the ears. Then AGE was given orally at 0, 4 and 15 hours later (once or three times at each given test hour).

AGE was at peak effectiveness four hours after picryl chloride was applied to the ears. The reason? It takes several hours for T-lymphocytes (immune cells) to release chemical messengers (cytokines) that cause inflammatory cells to arrive at the site of the allergen. Inasmuch as AGE was most effective at the fourth hour, the researchers conclude that it may inhibit the production or release of chemical messengers that cause allergic cascade reactions. [3]

"These results suggest that AGE applications could modify, directly or indirectly, the function of mast cells, basophils and activated T lymphocytes, which play a leading role in allergic cascade reactions, including inflammation." [4]

Garlic Versus Arthritis

Sometimes you may experience joint pains that seem like arthritis but may be an allergic reaction. D.N. Golding, M.D., a rheumatologist at Princess Alexandra Hospital in Harlow, Essex, England discovered what he calls "allergic synovitis". The synovial membrane in all the body's joint areas secretes a fluid that lubricates cavities containing joints. Nearby areas become inflamed from various allergies. [5]

Studying garlic's influence on cardiovascular disorders, medical researchers in India noted something unusual. Patients who ate two to three raw or cooked garlic cloves daily were often relieved of joint pain from osteoarthritis. These researchers theorized that garlic helps to produce prostaglandins, short term controllers of body processes, some of which reverse inflammation. Garlic versus arthritis is an area that will attract more researchers. [6]

Roy Kupsinel, M.D., of Oviedo, Florida. a well-known alternative physician, told the authors of his experiences with mineral imbalances, heavy metal intoxications and allergies to foods, chemicals and inhalants that could cause high blood pressure and arthritis.

"Hair analysis is an excellent diagnostic tool to measure minerals in the body. High levels of copper, iron, cadmium and lead may be seen in an arthritic trend. An allergen, a substance perceived as foreign to the body, may cause this condition as well as many others, ranging from bed-wetting and hyperactivity to schizophrenia.

"One food family, the nightshades – tomatoes, eggplant, peppers and tobacco – have definitely caused arthritis. A patient of mine has an allergy to saccharine that precipitates acute attacks of arthritis.

"Kyolic, aged garlic, is a major basic supplement in my nutritional-preventive medicine practice. Kyolic chelates or claws and binds toxic, heavy metals such as cadmium and lead. Garlic has the highest level of selenium in all the vegetable kingdom. Since selenium antagonizes heavy metals, selenium-rich Kyolic may further help cleanse the system of these toxins. Kyolic has been shown to protect experimental animals against the toxicity of sodium cyclamate and the adverse effects of food additives on growth." [7]

Probing The Mysteries of Alzheimer's Disease

Before indicating what garlic can do for Alzheimer's disease, it is important to describe this disorder and then probe the mystery of its causes. First memory goes. Then judgment becomes impaired, followed by sharp personality and temperament changes: irritability, quick temper, anxiety, depression and nervousness. Difficulty in thinking and remembering often trigger irritability. Physical deterioration devastates patients even more, because they can't take care of themselves. Inability to control their bladder or bowel shatters their dignity – particularly being cleaned up and diapered like a baby.

Over a four to eight year period, symptoms worsen until previously feared death often seems merciful. What causes Alzheimer's disease? There are almost as many theories as there are theorizers. Let's deal with the major ones. Some claim it's just the aging process. However, most seniors never develop characteristic symptoms other than a mild memory loss. Some claim it's the manifestation of chronic malnourishment. Still others believe it's an attack on brain cells by free radicals without enough antioxidants to counteract them.

One theory that refuses to go away is that it's a reaction to environmental pollution – particularly from aluminum. Autopsies of Alzheimer patients reveal aluminum at the sites of tangled neurofibrils (minute brain nerve fibers) and patches of beta amyloid, a waxy and toxic substance that comes from degenerated body tissue. Is aluminum a cause – possibly **the** cause – or a byproduct of the disease process?

As long ago as 35 years, Dr. D. Crapper at the University of Toronto, performed many autopsies on the brains of Alzheimer's disease patients and found aluminum there. Then he injected small amounts of aluminum into the brains of healthy lab animals. Soon, tangled neurofibrils, amyloid deposits and aluminum invariably appeared there. [8]

Aluminum: A Prime Suspect

How does aluminum enter the body? We invite it in many processed foods, in: fruits and vegetables grown in soils with a high level of aluminum, in free-flowing salt, some white flour, baking powder, some salad dressings and drinks in aluminum cans and many medicines and toiletries, as listed in the previous chapter.

The South Pacific island of Guam presents a frightening medical statistic. Almost 10 percent of its local population dies of a degenerative brain disease – Lou Gehrig's disease, Parkinsonism or another form of dementia. This is attributed to the high amount of aluminum in its soils. In a comparative study involving two nearby islands — Palau and Jamaica, which report only token degenerative disease — Guam was shown to have 42 times as much aluminum in its soils as the others. Nineteen of the most common foods eaten in Guam showed elevated levels of aluminum. So did the Guam drinking water. [9]

Although not nearly at as high a level as in Guam, most city water suppliers use alum to settle sediment.

A 10-year study of 4,000 40 to 69 year old volunteers in relation to aluminum in drinking water in 88 counties in England and Wales revealed that individuals drinking water containing the most aluminum were found to have a 50 percent greater chance of developing Alzheimer's disease than those who drink water without aluminum. [10]

The Revealing Snowden Study

The 15-year study of nuns in the order The School Sisters of Notre Dame in Mankato, Minnesota by epidemiologist David Snowdon, Ph.D, of the University of Kentucky's Sanders-Brown Center on Aging, revealed factors making the sisters Alzheimer's disease-prone: working in convent support jobs – cooking, housecleaning and clerical work — rather than in stimulating teaching – not continuing mind-enhancing functions such as reading, writing, issue-discussing and not consciously reversing negative thinking. Physical causes were having suffered strokes or head injuries and showing a deficiency of folic acid and the anti-oxidant lycopene in their bloodstream.

Dr. Snowdon told *Time* magazine this: "My epidemiology training is that there are hardly any diseases where one factor alone, even in infectious disease, will always cause illness." [11]

One of the few studies of aged garlic in relation to Alzheimer's disease was conducted by researchers at Oakwood College, Huntsville, Alabama, who wanted to know if aged garlic extract can protect nerve cells that degenerate in Alzheimer's disease. The researchers write that beta amyloid is a well-known poison that attacks brain nerves and starts free radical attacks. In a test-tube experiment, they pitted aged garlic against beta amyloid in brain nerve cells and found that, indeed, aged garlic protects against beta-amyloid poisoning in a dose-dependent manner. They concluded that "aged garlic may be useful in lessening Alzheimer's disease symptoms." [12]

Favorable Indications For Garlic

A second study by the same researchers two years later validated the first study, demonstrating that aged garlic guards against Alzheimer's disease by means of its antioxidant, anti-aging, and anti-ischemic factors.

Due to the fact that garlic strengthens immune function, it seems reasonable that it may help AIDS patients to delay or overcome their afflictions that come from weakened immunity and live longer.

The experiments of Florida pathologist Tariq Abdullah, MD, offer more than a little hope of this. Dr. Abdullah tested three groups of non-AIDS patients to determine effects of garlic on natural killer cells. Natural killer cells specialize in destroying virus-infected cells, other foreign invaders and cancer cells. [13]

For three weeks, one group took the equivalent of eight cloves of raw garlic daily. Another took six capsules of Kyolic 100 and the third took no garlic. Prior to the study, Dr. Abdullah checked the killer cell activity of each group against tumor cells in test tubes and found them almost equal. After three weeks, he again tested their killer cell activity and found startling differences. Killer cells of the group on raw garlic destroyed 140 percent more malignant cells than those of the control group. Killer cells of those on Kyolic aged garlic destroyed 160 percent more tumor cells than those of the control group! Kyolic proved to be more effective than raw garlic. Reporting his findings, Dr. Abdullah stated that aged garlic taken for three weeks will not only strengthen natural killer cells, but also supercharge the entire immune system. Encouraged, he wanted to test it on AIDS patients, noted for their compromised immune system. Negligible killer cell activity in AIDS patients leads to steady deterioration of their condition.

Develops More Killer Cells

Dr. Abdullah placed seven AIDS patients with subnormal killer cell activity on 12 weeks of Kyolic aged garlic extract supplementation. Six weeks later, five of the seven showed a dramatic rise in killer cell activity to normal range. After the 12th week, every patient showed normal range killer cell activity and a significant improvement in total immune system function.

The aged garlic supplement also promoted a sharp improvement in these patients' symptoms related to immune system suppression: diarrhea, Candida yeast overgrowth in the mouth and throat, infection of all the sinuses and recurrent genital herpes. Does Dr. Abdullah believe that aged garlic can cope with the human immunodeficiency virus (HIV) that causes AIDS?

He agrees it has promise, because it annihilates "a broad spectrum of disease-carrying microorganisms – viruses, bacteria, protozoa and yeasts." However, he wants to see results from far larger research projects for more conclusive answers.

He writes that "no substance, either natural or synthetic, can match garlic's proven therapeutic versatility and effectiveness."

Best Defenses Against HIV

One of the world's leading garlic researchers, Benjamin Lau, MD, PhD, professor of microbiology and Immunology at Loma Linda University School of Medicine, writes "Not long ago, a medical student working with me found that human immunodeficiency virus (HIV) or AIDS virus does not grow well in the presence of garlic in tissue culture. The possibilities of garlic are staggering!" [14]

Dr. Lau also writes that free radical attacks on T lymphocytes (key players in the immune system) weaken them so that HIV can damage them. [15]

Acknowledging that many people justifiably fear HIV, Dr. Lau tells us that our condition of health, lifestyle, nutrition, and immune status can either defend us against this disease or leave us defenseless. These things can demolish our defenses – toxic exposures such as recreational drugs and prescription and over-the-counter drugs that weaken our immunity and severe trauma. [16]

Aged garlic can help to prevent AIDS, as indicated by numerous studies, insists Dr. Lau. "Garlic can inhibit the growth of viruses, garlic enhances the function of phagocytes and natural killer cells, and garlic nullifies some of the toxins that impair the immune system. Viruses are parasites in the true sense, as they are incapable of reproducing themselves."

"When a virus enters a cell, it uses its genes to direct the cell to produce more viruses. To do so, viral genes must first be expressed. Our latest studies have revealed that garlic compounds can suppress the process of gene expression in the test tube, most likely through its antioxidant actions. If this suppression can happen in the body, there will be no viral growth."

One of the most sensational developments centers around a study done in India, indicating that even the devastating and incurable disease, leprosy, has been successfully treated with garlic. Conventional drugs to slow the spread of this ailment are so distasteful that many leprosy patients have said, "I would rather die than continue on this medicine." Now there is hope that garlic may give them a positive alternative." [17]

Chapter 3

New Weapon Against TB, Sickle Cell Anemia and Ulcers

Three difficult-to-manage, serious ailments may have met their match in aged garlic: tuberculosis (TB), sickle cell anemia, and stomach ulcers that could cause cancer. Recently, when even powerful antibiotics failed to stop T.B, an old scourge became a new scourge, a highly infectious ailment again rapidly spreading worldwide. An organism called Myobacterium tuberculosis attacks the lungs in between 80 and 90 percent of the cases, and, in some, the intestinal tract, the lymph glands, the bones, the brain and the skin.

Highly contagious, TB can be spread by a cough in the rebreathed air of an airplane, a train, subway car, bus, a crowded meeting room, an auditorium or in dormitories. This warning is intended as a wake up call, not a scare tactic.

Early in the last century, TB patients were isolated for months in sanitariums for two good reasons: to offer them a maximum opportunity to heal – with bed rest, moderate exercise, fresh air, some exposure to sunlight and a highly nutritious diet — and a minimum opportunity to spread the disease. Today astronomical hospital and convalescent home costs rule out long stays and a treatment that was slow but usually effective. Now, except in deathbed cases, TB patients take their moderately helpful antibiotics at home. Meanwhile everyone there is exposed to and threatened by TB and may carry the microorganism to the public.

Simon Martin, an award-winning British health writer-editor, reports that critics of orthodox medicine have protested, for more than a decade, against the over-use of antibiotics and the frightening danger from tuberculosis and other contagious diseases. However, the spread of antibiotic-resistant bacteria is threatening both there and in the United States. [1]

Stop Antibiotics for Animal Growth

The United Kingdom has asked the European Union to control the use of antibiotics for promoting growth and increased weight of meat animals, "a practice that has helped create animal reservoirs of antibiotic-resistant bacteria."

"All our farm animals are regularly dosed with antibiotics, not just for infections, but also as growth promoters. More than 40 percent of antibiotics manufactured in the U.S. are given to animals," writes Martin. "In America, a study at Rutgers University found that antibiotics used at levels deemed safe for human consumption by the U.S. Food and Drug Administration increased the rate of development of resistant bacteria by 500-2,700 per cent."

Martin quotes biochemist Nigel Plummer, PhD: "The normal flora of the gut are important in preventing infections, but antibiotics can have a devastating effect on them, sometimes completely eliminating them. Probiotics may well play a very important role in reestablishing normal flora." Only garlic enhances the multiplication of friendly bacteria.

The problem rises high above people popping antibiotic pills to prevent infection and counter the slightest scratch or cut. Tuberculosis and pneumonia are once more becoming killer diseases for another reason cited by Martin. Hospitals are colonized by bacteria resistant to almost all drugs that used to stop them dead. A World Health Organization (WHO) source claims that harmful microorganisms are developing resistance to antibiotics faster than drug companies can develop new ones, making the threat of a 21st century plague almost inevitable.

An Answer to the Problem

One of the best opponents of TB is aged garlic. When garlic meets TB, garlic usually wins. This has been so since early in the last century, much to the surprise of today's patients and physicians. Courageous and creative doctors at that time pioneered the use of garlic for TB patients and, in most cases, helped them, continues Martin.

Early 20th century, pioneer doctors, inspired by the success of garlic with supposedly incurable lung disease in ancient Egypt, Babylon, Phoenicia and China – among countless other ailments – first used garlic for seemingly hopeless cases. One of them, W.C. Minchin, MD, practiced medicine in the TB ward of Kells Hospital in Dublin. The other, M.W. McDuffie, MD, of the Metropolitan Hospital in New York City, specialized in treating TB patients. [2]

Finding that conventional therapy was sometimes ineffective against this number one killer, Dr. Minchin felt strongly that garlic would cure it, so he solicited hopeless cases from other doctors and got the patients' permission to try this (then) experimental treatment.

Patients improved so rapidly that doctors who had given them only a few weeks or months to live marveled and wanted to know how he did it. Dr. Minchin, at first, refused to divulge his secret, because, even in those days, doctors were under pressure to use only conventional treatments. However, once enough patients regained full health, he told their doctors that he had had them take raw garlic internally, breathe its fumes, and apply garlic ointment and compresses to their skin above the lungs or any other body part afflicted with TB.

Some tubercular children responded positively to raw garlic rubbed on the soles of their feet. Garlic travels with near lightning speed in the body, so the young patients had garlic breath within seconds. Unless cured rapidly, these children either lost their hearing or their lives.

Convincing Case Histories

Dr. Minchin then revealed his cure in articles in the British medical publication *Lancet*, and soon his office was landslided with letters from doctors worldwide who congratulated him and shared their own experiences with garlic therapy and TB.

In one article, he summed up these responses as follows:

"The peasants and farmers in the area have always used garlic as a cure for tuberculosis, coughs, colds, intestinal and digestive disorders, boils and even poisoning. Perhaps this was not just superstition. Perhaps they are wiser than we know."

Here are brief summaries of some of his typical TB cases. A 10-year old boy with tuberculosis of the hand was admitted to Kells hospital for an amputation. Dr. Minchin couldn't stand the thought of someone so young needlessly losing a hand, so he took the case, treating the boy with many daily garlic compresses. Within six weeks, the hand was completely healed.

A 15 year old girl had TB infection in all of her neck glands and beneath her jaw, a condition regarded by her doctor as hopeless. Dr. Minchin took the case, had her eat raw garlic many times a day and apply garlic compresses to her neck. She was improved within a week and fully cured in six months.

Dr. Minchin established a precedent for those times – outpatient treatment for lung TB. Patients consumed much raw garlic, and, home in the evening, inhaled garlic and applied garlic compresses. His total cures astonished fellow doctors.

Toughest Cases

Old records are not clear as to whether an American doctor, W.M. McDuffie, MD, of the Metropolitan Hospital in New York City, had read publications of Dr. Minchin or had discovered the garlic TB treatment on his own. No mild cases were admitted to his ward. "Practically every case is a stretcher case, and the majority die within a few days or weeks," he wrote.

In a publication in the *North American Journal of Homeopathy* for May, 1914, Dr. McDuffie described his treatments for 1082 patients with 56 different modalities – from hydrochloric acid to chest surgery to garlic. Summarizing results, he concluded:

"Garlic is the best individual treatment found to get rid of germs, and we believe it to be a specific for the tubercle bacillus and for tubercular processes no matter what part of the body is affected, whether skin, bones, glands, lungs or special parts. Thus, by diet, rest, and exercise, baths and climate, garlic furnishes sufficient and specific treatment for the medical aspects of this disease."

The last sentence of this nearly 90-year old quotation sounds new in the mouths of today's holistic doctors who know that treatment with antibiotics – no matter how powerful — is far from successful in coping with the growing TB epidemic. The antibiotic approach is just a single solution — one leg of what should be a tripod. This is why it topples.

Fight TB Three Ways

The holistic approach, best described by Benjamin Lau, MD, Ph.D, professor of microbiology and immunology at Loma Linda University School of Medicine, and world authority on garlic, involves the tri-phase treatment: (1) disabling harmful microorganisms (2) strengthening the immune function, and (3) minimizing or eliminating immune-crippling stress: environmental poisons, physical trauma and emotional tension.

Garlic is programmed to kill TB – many other microorganisms, too – without damaging friendly bacteria, something that is not true about antibiotics that slaughter indiscriminately and sometimes bring along harmful side effects.

In his classic book, *Garlic and You* (Apple Publishing) Dr.

Lau claims that: microorganisms alone do not usually cause infection **unless there is a susceptible host."** A third factor is some form of stress, as mentioned earlier.

Garlic is phenomenal in that it strengthens all three legs of the tripod: (1) annihilating TB bacteria and many other microorganisms; (2) revving up the immune system and (3) helping to ward off the negative affects of stress.

A frightening development today is the continuing ability of enemy microorganisms to attack us despite the use of antibiotics that once killed them. There's good reason to believe that garlic can handle these challenges without harm to the bodies it is protecting.

The James Duke Approach

Let's take a quick look at a study that makes this very point. Researchers at Boston City Hospital had difficulty finding antibiotics that would cure ear infections of children. Swabbing their throats and noses, the scientists removed 14 individual families of bacteria. In a lab experiment, aged garlic extract killed every one of the strains, including those that resisted antibiotics. [3]

In *The Green Pharmacy*, James A. Duke, PhD, one of the world's foremost authorities on medicinal plants and herbs, writes that about one percent of new TB cases in New York City are caused by bacteria resistant to one antibiotic. Up to seven percent of recurrent cases are resistant to two or more antibiotics. TB patients resistant to multiple antibiotics have only a 50 percent chance of surviving. [4]

"The Chinese use garlic to treat TB with decent results," writes Dr. Duke. "If I feared that I'd been exposed to TB, I would take at least one garlic capsule a day, and I'd make sure the label said that each capsule was standardized to the equivalent of at least one gram of fresh garlic."

About Sickle Cell Anemia

An even more difficult challenge to therapy than TB is sickle cell anemia, a serious ailment that afflicts one out of every 500 blacks in the United States. This disorder causes some red blood cells to change from their usual oval shape to a sickle shape and congeal, blocking microcirculation so that tissue starves for lack of oxygen and nutrients, causing fever, joint and severe abdominal pains and, sometimes, jaundice, as well as early death. Sickled cells live a short life, and blood, deficient in red blood cells, brings on anemia.

Added to the harm caused by their unorthodox shape, sickle cells have leaky membranes, which cause them to lose fluid, become dense and sticky and adhere to cells lining blood vessels. Oxidation, too, contributes to this undermining process.

Sickle cell anemia is inherited. If one parent carries this trait genetically, the child generally does not acquire this ailment unless he or she is seriously oxygen-deprived, as in anesthesia. However, if both parents carry this gene, sickle cell anemia **is inevitable.**

The late Nobel Laureate Dr. Linus Pauling discovered, in 1950, that a chemical abnormality in the blood's hemoglobin – the oxygen-carrying substance – causes red blood cells to become deformed.

Now there's strong hope that more can be done for sickle cell anemia patients than kill the pain. In lab experiments, Dr. T. Onishi, of the Philadelphia Biomedical Research Institute, found that sickle cells that accumulate and cause blockage in blood vessels can be kept from forming by S-allyl cysteine (SAC), an antioxidant in aged garlic extract. He also announced that sickle cell anemia patients reveal low levels of vitamin E, so that this vitamin and other antioxidants might well team up with garlic to reduce chances of blood vessel blockage. [5]

A Possible New Therapy

Fifty years after Dr. Linus Pauling identified sickle cell anemia as the first example of a molecular disease, biochemists S. Tsuyoshi Ohnishi and Tomoko Ohnishi, in a paper, "In Vitro effects of Aged Garlic Extract and Other Nutritional Supplements on Sickle Erythrocytes," presented to a Newport Beach, California Garlic Conference, reported that "sickle cell anemia is now further proposed to be an example of 'a membrane-linked disease,' and a new nutritional therapy is proposed.

"The recipe employs none other than the antioxidants which Pauling so ardently advocated at the latter stage of his career. These nutritional supplements would be safer than any other drugs tested to date on sickle cell patients."

A pilot clinical trial by the Onishi research group to determine if aged garlic and other antioxidants could reduce the amount of dense cell formation showed promise. Over six months, these biochemists demonstrated that 6 grams of aged garlic extract – a gram is 1/28th of an ounce – 4 to 6 grams of vitamin C and 800 to 1200 I.U. of vitamin E daily may be beneficial to sickle cell patients in that it improved blood values and showed a trend toward reducing painful crises. [6]

How effective are anti-oxidants such as SAC in aged garlic? Biochemist P.G. Pietta, MD, told the same garlic conference that they inhibit free radicals from injuring fatty portions of cells in rats and ultimately cutting off blood circulation to the brain. [7]

In other research on sickle cell blockage of blood flow, N. Numagami, of the Philadelphia Biomedical Research Institute, found that treatment of rats with S-allyl-cysteine (SAC), before blood flow restriction – and the explosion of free radicals when the flow of oxygenated blood is restored, improved their health, limited swelling and enhanced memory and performance. [8]

Dealing With Another Complication

Oxidation of red blood cells causes another harmful complication in sickle cell anemia, the development of Heinz bodies, substances that stick to membranes of hemoglobin and damage them. As a defense mechanism, red blood cells attacked by Heinz bodies are removed from the bloodstream by shunting them to the spleen for disposal. However, this valuable service may also turn out to be a disservice, because the removal of needed red blood cells can cause anemia.

To cope with this phenomenon, researchers at UCLA conducted a four-week clinical study and found that one teaspoonful of liquid aged garlic extract daily significantly reduced the forming of Heinz bodies. Their conclusion? That aged garlic slashes oxidation and, therefore, may protect sickle red blood cells and lessen the complications of sickle cell anemia. [9]

Research by biochemist Harunobu Amagase, PhD, of Wakunaga of America, with various antioxidants derived from aged garlic led to developing a product promising for coping with sickle cell anemia. It has been so successful in vitro and animal studies that the U.S. government granted the company a patent for it as specific for this medical ailment. [10]

Down with Ulcers

Far more prevalent and far less dangerous than sickle cell anemia is a condition called ulcers, crater-like erosions in the protective mucus in the stomach or duodenum, the start of the small intestine. However, an estimated 10 percent of the population develops this condition that causes pain shortly before a meal or three or four hours after.

A breakdown of mucus permits digestive juices to attack the stomach or duodenum lining. For decades, a cliché attributed such ulcers to stress – and this can be a secondary cause – in "it's not what you eat, but what's eating you." This viewpoint has been modified in the last several decades. Now, most ulcers have been found to be caused by a microorganism called Helicobacter pylori.

One of the best bets for this condition is vitamin C – generally 1,000 mg taken twice daily, as recommended by many alternative doctors. A Bastyr University researcher, Gowsala P. Sivam, ND, studied the anti-bacterial power of garlic for 10 years – 1975 to 1985 — and it turns out to be Murder Incorporated against numerous causes of disease – salmonella, typhimurium, E coli, kliebella, and, among many others, staphylococcus. [11]

There's more to fear from stomach ulcers caused by Helicobacter pylori than just pain: the possibility of cancer. Dr. Sivam conducted experiments demonstrating that aged garlic extract killed the Helicobacter pylori in test tubes. And she stated that as little as one clove of garlic might be enough to kill this organism in a human being.

This news rates screaming headlines in that 122 out of 145 patients infected with Helicobacter pylori got no help from antibiotics that were supposed to kill this organism,states Dr. Sivam. [12]

W.C. You, MD, representing the National Cancer Institute, revealed results of a fascinating study of Helicobacter pylori in patients in Cangshan County, China. The prevalence of this organism in their stomach was in direct proportion to the degree of stomach damage. He found Helicobacter pylori in 19 percent of those with healthy stomach lining; in 35 percent of those with superficial gastritis (inflammation of the stomach lining); in 56% of those with chronic atrophic gastritis (inflammation and wasting- away tissues); in 80 percent with intestinal metaplasia (changing character of the stomach lining); and 100 percent with abnormal cell growth. [13]

Dr. You stated that eating garlic showed protective effects of the stomach lining and a marked decline of H pylori infection.

Chapter 4

Supplemental Insurance for Heart and Arteries

Every biochemist names one or more of the following as the major cause of heart and circulatory system ailments: high blood cholesterol levels, too much low density lipoprotein, excessive blood triglycerides; too much lipoprotein (a); excessive homocysteine in the blood, abnormal blood clotting, high blood pressure, too few antioxidants to cope with free radicals and incessant stress.

And stacks of studies back the validity of each one. That heart of yours beats 70 times a minute – more than 100,000 times a day – to pump oxygen-laden blood and nutrients to your trillions of cells with no time off for good behavior. How well and how long that big pump and your circulatory system – veins, arteries and capillaries — stay in good shape is up to one person –YOU!

There are individual solutions for every one of the causes named. However, there's a single solution for all of them that towers over others like the highest mountain peak over the lowest valley – garlic. Let's consider major causes, starting with cholesterol readings.

A dramatic experiment by cardiologists Drs. Arun Bordia and H. C. Bansal, in India, tests the effects of a saturated fat on cholesterol levels and spotlights the power of garlic. The researchers fed a quarter of a pound of butter at one time to five healthy volunteers. Within three hours, their cholesterol levels rose from an average of 221.4 to 237.4 – not a terrifying increase, but still an increase. [1]

At a later date, these biochemists fed the volunteers the same amount of butter. However, this time they added two capsules containing 50 grams of garlic juice – less than two ounces. Within three hours, instead of rising, cholesterol levels of the volunteers dropped from 228,7 to 212.7. Is this an invitation for you to eat your popcorn floating on melted butter or your bread with half an inch of butter trowelled on? No way! It's just an illustration of the protective powers of garlic.

Shocked at Results

Excited about positive results that aged, odorless garlic had on cholesterol and triglyceride levels of several doctors' patients, Benjamin Lau, MD, Ph.D., professor of microbiology and immunology at Loma Linda University, and associates, conducted a three-part clinical study of 32 volunteers with cholesterol readings of 220 to 440 to determine the influence of aged garlic extract on levels of blood fats. [2]

Half the group received four capsules of Kyolic liquid garlic extract daily, and the other half took caramel-colored, look-alike placebos. Blood lipids were measured each month, and, after the second month, Dr. Lau got such a shock that he almost abandoned the study. Volunteers taking the garlic showed an increase in blood cholesterol and triglycerides. Placebo-takers registered no change.

Simultaneously, he learned that Dr. Arun Bordia had seen the same results after two months in a similar study with patients taking fresh garlic daily. Rather than interpret this as a bad sign, Dr. Bordia saw it as a gain for the patients. Garlic appeared to be moving lipids from tissues, including the liver and arteries, where they had accumulated, into the bloodstream where they eventually were thrown off in body wastes. Then after the third month, blood fats declined. [3]

Similar results occurred in a U.S. Department of Agriculture Nutrition Institute study with rats fed garlic extract. After two months of supplementation, they had more lipids in their blood but less in their liver. [4]

Continuing his study, Dr. Lau found a significant drop in his high-cholesterol volunteers' blood lipids after the third month and lipid levels approaching normal values after six months. [5]

Subsequent animal studies repeated these results and verified the findings of Drs. Bordia and Lau. [6]

Validation

A second part of the Lau experiment – this time with subjects in the normal blood lipid range — produced almost identical results – a mild rise in blood cholesterol and triglycerides after two months, then a drop. [7]

A final part of the study – this with patients high in cholesterol and triglycerides — revealed a rise in blood fats after two months on four capsules daily of aged garlic extract. Then, after three months, 65 percent of patients on the garlic experienced a significant decline in blood fat levels. Why only 65 percent? Dr. Lau wondered, too, until interviews revealed that the remaining 35 percent regularly gorged on fatty meats such as steaks, a lot of pastries and rich ice cream – especially during the evening meal — processed food high in oxidized cholesterol, and drank beer and hard liquor, which readily turn to cholesterol and fat.

When patients reduced their intake of such foods and alcohol and continued on the garlic supplement, their blood lipids plunged, too.

This study also showed that low density lipoprotein (LDL) and very low density lipoprotein (VLDL) – extremely harmful cholesterol – decreased significantly after the third month with a rapid rise in high density lipoprotein (HDL) – the good cholesterol – a favorable trend that became even more favorable after the sixth month. [8]

Researchers at the University of Oxford in England analyzed 30 published papers about blood lipids, including that by Dr. Lau, and found that garlic supplements over a period of three or more months were beneficial in protecting against cardiovascular disorders. [9]

Acknowledging the importance of cholesterol levels, biochemists strongly accent the need for having sufficient antioxidants to quench free radicals that result from the oxidation of low density lipoproteins. Oxidized LDL damages cells lining blood vessels by changing macrophages (immune system cells) into foam cells that readily stick to them. Dr. Lau and his Loma Linda University research team found that aged garlic protects the integrity of blood vessels in two ways: guarding LDL against oxidation and preventing oxidized LDL from damaging cell membranes or killing cells. [10]

Benefits without Side Effects

Many doctors consider anti-cholesterol drugs the total answer to cardiovascular complications. It isn't. They sometimes invite horrendous side effects, including negative emotions, hostility, aggression and depression. One of the statin drugs killed more than 100 individuals before the Food and Drug Administration banned its use. Various authorities maintain that only one person in 500 – one with familial hypercholesterolemia – needs to follow a Spartan diet so far as fats and cholesterol are concerned and to take cholesterol-lowering medication. Many studies demonstrate that daily exercise such as walking for 30 minutes can lower elevated cholesterol. Many tests show that aged garlic lowers cholesterol safely.

Some publications reveal that Kyolic aged garlic extract also protects arteries and other body parts from the ravages of free radical attacks by boosting the activity of antioxidant enzymes such as glutathione and superoxide dismutase. Kyolic also blocks the growth of smooth muscle cells over scar tissue that reduces the flow through blood vessels and lessens chances of atherosclerosis developing. [11]

Some years ago, Dr. Anthony Verlangieri, while at Rutgers

University, created an artificial vitamin C shortage in rabbits and proved that this caused their normally smooth artery linings to lose certain chemical compounds, creating irregularities, ideal places for harmful plaques to accumulate. A generous intake of vitamin C assured that these chemical compounds stayed where they belong, making for smooth artery linings. [12]

Dr. Verlangieri's findings were validated by 22 years of experiments by Dr. M. L. Riccitelli, of the Yale School of Medicine. [13]

Still Another Theory

Lipoprotein (a) is still another cause of reduced capacity for blood flow in arteries, maintains Matthias Rath, M. D., based on his research at the Linus Pauling Heart Institute, where he made this discovery. When there's not enough vitamin C to synthesize collagen that helps to keep artery interiors smooth and strong, lipoprotein (a) acts as an instant repair kit to seal weak areas. However, the repair creates roughness or even small craters where biochemical debris collects and slows or blocks blood flow.

"Heart attack and stroke are essentially unknown in animals producing vitamin C in their bodies," writes Dr. Rath. "In human beings, dependent on dietary vitamin C and frequently having a low intake of this vitamin, heart disease is a leading cause of disability or death. Vitamin C stimulates the production of collagen molecules, which play the same role in the human body that steel reinforcement plays in a skyscraper. Heart disease is a form of pre-scurvy. Heart attack and stroke are a direct result of low vitamin C intake over the years." [14]

Dr. Pauling had a novel way of stressing our special needs for vitamin C, because human beings cannot synthesize this nutrient. During his talks, he would hold up three vials before the audience. The first was filled with considerable powdered vitamin C. "This is how much vitamin C a jackass makes in his body in a 24-hour period."

Holding up the second vial with only an infinitesimal amount of this nutrient, he said, "This is the amount of vitamin C the Food and Drug Administration says we need. Then holding up the third vial, which was empty, he said, "This is the amount we human beings make in a 24-hour period, which proves that a jackass knows more about vitamin C than the FDA."

The Persecution of Dr. McCully

Although garlic contains vitamin C, no valid study shows that it supplies enough of this vitamin to keep artery interiors healthy and smooth. However, much research demonstrates that it enhances the power and value of vitamin C.

Another enemy to arteries and the heart is a substance called homocysteine, a byproduct of the breakdown of the amino acid methionine. Discovery of the hazards of homocysteine by researcher Kilmer McCully, M. D., while at Harvard University, flew in the face of current medical thought and led to Harvard dismissing him. McCully had to fight a long and tough battle against resistance to his theory by other medical researchers and the medical profession, wedded until death do us part, to cholesterol and blood fats as the only causes of cardiovascular diseases.

Now, finally, elevated homocysteine is widely accepted as a threat to arteries and the heart. Tobacco smoking, excessive drinking of alcohol, heavy caffeine intake, oral contraceptives, menopause and nutritional deficiency are noted for decreasing the enzymes that convert homocysteine to a harmless substance.

At this writing, some 80 clinical and population studies back the McCully findings that homocysteine damages cells that line the inside of veins and arteries, stimulating the harmful growth of smooth muscle cells over injured areas. [15]

The Homocysteine Story

Homocysteine sabotages the circulatory system in other ways, too. It activates blood-clotting mechanisms and fails to shut them off, increasing the risk of blood stoppage and strokes, as well as heart attacks. It also makes LDL, Bad Guy cholesterol, even worse, causing it to form particles that are taken up by macrophages – PAC-man type immune cells – that turn into foam cells that etch and scar the interior of veins and arteries like a strong acid. [16]

Numerous studies show that vitamins B-6, B-12 and folic acid are a **must** for making potent homocysteine impotent. Now animal research – this by Dr. Y. Yeh at Pennsylvania State University – reveals that, in the absence of sufficient folic acid, the most powerful biochemical force against homocysteine, aged garlic extract, reduces blood homocysteine by 30 percent. Dr. Yeh states, "Aged garlic extract used in the study effectively reduced hyper-homocysteinemia caused by severe folate deficiency." [17]

In numerous public statements, Susan Lark, a prominent medical doctor, warns that "women with high levels of homocysteine have 24 times the risk of heart disease than those whose levels are low."

An eminent physician and clinical researcher who advocates the use of aged garlic to reduce high blood levels of homocysteine is Gary Gordon, MD, D.O., cofounder of the American College for the Advancement in Medicine and president of Gordon Research in Payson, Arizona. [18]

"We doctors may have to show a little humility toward nature's most versatile and therapeutic herb, garlic," he says. "Why? Because the United States Patents and Trade Mark Office has granted a usage patent to the makers of odorless Kyolic Aged Garlic Extract (AGE) for reducing elevated homocysteine levels."

To illustrate this patent's importance, Dr. Gordon points to a five-year follow-up study of 14,916 doctors, which showed a threefold increase in heart attacks for those with the highest levels of homocysteine. Dr. Gordon believes it will soon be common practice for doctors to pay more attention to their patients' homocysteine levels than to their cholesterol levels.

He highlights three specific benefits – over and above lowering homocysteine levels — that come with aged garlic extract (AGE): (1) aging changes garlic from a strong, odoriferous, oxidizing agent to an odorless and potent antioxidant cell protector; (2) AGE prevents the oxidation of serum cholesterol and (3) It stimulates blood circulation and has a blood-thinning effect, reducing the multiple risk factors of cardiovascular diseases.

Superior to Aspirin

Equally important as the good health and interior smoothness of arteries is the condition of the blood. Blood that clots abnormally can block blood flow and cause strokes, heart attacks and many other serious or killing diseases. Most doctors recommend an aspirin a day to keep the blood fluid. Unfortunately this is only a partial answer to a many-headed problem and often brings along the side effect of bleeding in the stomach and elsewhere. An aspirin cannot cope with blood fats and cholesterol, triglycerides, homocysteine and high blood pressure. It cannot keep the interior of arteries smooth.

Referring to seven prospective, randomized, placebo-controlled studies of 15,000 heart attack survivors taking anywhere from 325 mg to 1,500 mg of aspirin daily for from four weeks to five years, Drs. Michael Murray and Joseph Pizzorno state that "not a single study demonstrated a statistically significant reduction in mortality with aspirin." [19]

Numerous studies have demonstrated the effectiveness of aged garlic as a blood thinner that comes without side effects. Research of biochemist Dr. A. Qureshi at the University of Wisconsin demonstrates that thromboxane B-2 is one of the prime factors in clotting blood. And that aged garlic lowers elevated thromboxane B-2, as well as cholesterol and triglycerides. [20]

Professor Maurice Bennink, a biochemical researcher at Michigan State University for more than 17 years, verifies the Qureshi finding.

"The one thing that is very, very certain is the ability of garlic to reduce blood clotting. That is very well documented, as well as other things such as the reduction of blood lipids and especially, blood triglycerides and other cholesterol fractions."

Something significant on this subject that seems to be lost on most of the medical profession is a special kind of blood testing that reveals clots in time to dissolve them to prevent cardiovascular complications, disability and death.

More than 30 years ago, James R. Privatera, MD, a holistic practitioner in Covina, California, discovered an unorthodox but foolproof method of doing this by means of a low-cost technique, darkfield microscopy, that, for decades, was used almost exclusively for diagnosing syphilis. [21]

Dr. Privatera continues to invite physicians to protect their patients by learning from him how to apply the test and evaluate darkfield microscopy results. Except for some alternative doctors who have accepted and used it successfully, the test has been stonewalled. Dr. Privatera constantly urges hospital administrators to install this equipment in their emergency rooms for instant evaluation of patients stressed with chest pains, strokes or related medical conditions. Response has been negligible.

A drop of blood pinpricked from a patient's earlobe or finger is placed on a slide and put under a darkfield microscope, projecting the patient's live blood onto a TV monitor for review.

Clots readily stand out from normal blood cells, signaling the need for a blood-thinner and, once the patient is temporarily safe, for a change of lifestyle – vitamins, minerals, enzymes and blood-thinners such as aged garlic – and, later, a doctor-approved exercise program, and possibly chelation, a harmless, biochemical means of etching away arterial blockages.

In his alerting book, *Silent Clots,* written with Alan Stang, Dr. Privatera reveals the following:

"More than half of the deaths in America today are caused by heart attacks and strokes . . . When a clot occurs in the brain, interrupting blood flow, the resulting stroke, often kills part of the brain.

A stroke is major or minor, depending on the blood vessel where clots and blockage occur. Ninety percent of strokes are caused by clots."

Little known is the fact that clots may also contribute to cancer.

"With few exceptions, clots are involved in metastatic cancer," he warns. "Clots restrict oxygen, which encourages cancer cells to thrive. Clots also produce a substance called 'platelet derived growth factor' that suppresses the immune system, thus promoting the spread of cancer."

One of Dr. Privatera's driving forces in promoting darkfield microscopy is an incident that occurred years ago. A close friend was hospitalized with a severe, paralyzing stroke. Immediately upon hearing of this, he phoned the patient's cardiologist for permission to take and examine under darkfield microscopy the patient's blood. He was given permission.

A darkfield photo showed a huge clot fifteen to twenty times the size of a normal blood cell, indicating that there were similar clots in the bloodstream, which had probably caused the stroke. This was viewed by the head intensive care unit nurse, the chief lab technician and Dr. Privatera, who immediately told the attending internist and neurologist his finding, suggesting that they administer heparin, a potent, natural and commonly used blood-thinner.

His suggestion was turned down by both physicians, because, they claimed "It is not standard protocol to rely on darkfield examination for revealing the presence of clots."

A week later, the doctors administered heparin, but the patient soon died. Dr. Privatera concluded the story by saying:

"The heparin at that point (when he first recommended it) may or may not have extended life or increased the slim possibility of recovery. However, I felt that there was nothing to lose."

Doctors or patients who wish to reach Dr. Privatera can write, phone or FAX him as follows:

James R. Privatera, MD
105 North Grandview, Covina, CA 91723
Phone: (818) 966-1618 - FAX: (818) 966-7226

Lowering High Blood Pressure

Added to its ability to thin blood, garlic also has a way with another threat to heart and arteries – hypertension (high blood pressure). It helps to reduce systolic (pumping) and diastolic (heart resting) readings. Garlic has been used in China and Japan to treat hypertension for several hundred years, states an article in *American Pharmacy.* The Japanese Food and Drug Administration officially recognizes its efficacy for this purpose. [22]

If garlic were a human being, people would lay out a red carpet to welcome it – especially men, because conventional prescription drugs for high blood pressure often steal male potency, bringing along a side effect of frustration and acute depression.

Dr. Benjamin Lau writes that, since 1921, garlic has been shown to lower high blood pressure. He reports on a Chinese study in which 70 hypertensive patients were fed an average of one bulb of raw garlic daily with heartening results. Blood pressure of 33 patients dropped markedly. That of 14 dropped moderately, making the total success rate 61.7 percent. [23]

A study of hypertensive cats in Bulgaria spotlighted the greater value of aged garlic over fresh in managing high blood pressure. Blood pressure of cats injected with fresh garlic went down moderately. It plummeted when aged garlic was used. Aging seemed to enable certain enzyme processes to increase the power of pertinent biochemicals. [24]

The Inside Story

How does garlic cope with hypertension? One well-structured study shows that it can dilate blood vessels, easing the pressure. [25]

Other research reveals that garlic increases the potency of nitric oxide synthase, an enzyme that raises the level of nitric oxide in our body. Nitric oxide is well-documented for relaxing the smooth muscle in blood vessels and, therefore, lowering blood pressure. [26]

Dr. Lau likes to tell an anecdote about a patient who recommended that a neighbor with hypertension and high cholesterol above 300 try garlic along with his anti-cholesterol medication. The neighbor suffered more side effects than benefits from the conventional medicine, so he switched to aged garlic.

Several months later the man returned to his doctor, who was delighted that his patient's blood pressure was now normal and that his cholesterol had dropped to 220 for the first time in years. A couple months after that, the neighbor again had a check-up by his doctor. This time his cholesterol reading had dropped to 170.

Envious, the doctor, whose cholesterol was 240, said that he had better get on the medication. Then the patient had to confess that he was taking aged garlic. Instead of being upset with him, the doctor proved to be open-minded and tried garlic. After three months, his cholesterol reading had dropped to 160. At a meeting, the doctor told Dr. Lau that garlic had given him so much energy, he was able to cut out coffee!

Incredible Discovery

One of the major reasons for cardiovascular disorders is often minimized or ignored. That's stress: physical, emotional and mental. Too bad, because unceasing stress can be a killer. You should know what it does to your arteries. Alan C. Yeung, MD, a cardiologist at Harvard Medical School, studied 26 male and female volunteers who had chest pains symptomatic of coronary artery disease. [27]

Using angiography, a special X-ray technique, he viewed the subjects' three coronary arteries, the major blood vessels to the heart. Then he classified the condition of the artery interiors in three ways: (1) relatively smooth; (2) irregular (with a small amount of plaque) and stenosed (almost clogged with plaque).

Subjecting the patients to mental stress, he studied their coronary arteries and was amazed. Stress had caused the most plaqued arteries to narrow even more, reducing blood flow to the heart. This narrowing could have led to a heart attack. The most plaque-filled arteries tightened by 24 percent. Arteries with only little plaque constricted by nine percent. And – surprise! – smooth and healthy arteries showed no perceptible constriction.

To verify these findings further, Dr. Yeung tested results of the stress by means of blood flow. Sure enough, volume of blood flow decreased sharply – by 27 percent in both the mildly and extremely clogged arteries. In sharp contrast, it increased by 10 percent in the smooth arteries.

The reason? The smooth lining of healthy arteries can expand and permit the flow of more blood. When the hormone epinephrine – formerly called adrenaline – sends out a message for these vessels to constrict, the smooth lining of healthy blood vessels secretes a substance called endothelium-derived relaxing factor (EDRF).

"Healthy vessels secrete EDRF to balance the constricting effect of epinephrine," Yeung told the American Heart Association's 64th session. "But if you have unhealthy vessels, that balancing act is gone."

Watch Out for the Subtle Stressors!

There are a few things you should know about stress and keeping it from making you a candidate for a smorgasbord of physical, emotional and mental disorders. The subtle stressors are the ones that do most of the harm, because you may not be aware that they are sabotaging you.

Most physical stressors are obvious: major surgery, severe burns, a serious car accident, chemotherapy, crash diets, fasting, physical immobility, exhaustion, animal and snake bites, long exposure to extreme cold or heat, rarefied air, electric shock or radiation.

Not only because they are subtle, but because they endure, emotional stressors bleed us of energy and morale like a storage battery is drained as you keep your car's starter churning away when the ignition refuses to work. An army of psychologists agrees that these are the prime killers: grief over an important loss (the death of a loved one) endless frustration, being fired from a job, depression, mental illness, prolonged sickness of a family member (as in Alzheimer's disease), acute sexual problems, long-held grudges, anxiety, fear and, especially, hatred that corrodes like a burning acid.

These reduce our ability to digest, absorb and assimilate food and, even worse, cause a build-up of unused adrenal hormones. Physical threats motivate us to a "fight or flight" situation. Emotional ones do not. There's a continuous civil war being waged on the inside. So, as in all such campaigns, there's a war debt to be paid. That debt is insidious, chronic disease. Depleted of energy, one tends to overeat and add unwanted weight – another stress.

What are some of the major clues that emotional stressors are at work? Gritting or grinding of teeth, eyestrain and nervous blinking, high blood pressure, irregular and shallow breathing, tenseness, nervous jittering of knees when sitting, and feeling helpless.

Stress Breakers

In a phone conversation, Dr. Cary L. Cooper, of the University of Manchester (England) and a world authority on stress, told Jim Scheer, "Once you identify your stressors – and this is of paramount importance – you can cope with them. You pluck them out of your mind like weeds in your garden." There's a high price paid for resentment, hatred and grudges – in body, mind and emotions.

Dr. Cooper recommends daily exercise to release tensions and use up emotionally-stimulated hormone release. "Running, sauna, meditation and biofeedback all can help relieve stress. So can quiet relaxation coupled with deep breathing," he concluded.

Some of us struggle falling and staying asleep because we have unwelcome bedfellows – anxiety and worry. We can't drop the third act curtain. The day's events – mainly the negative ones — continue instant replays during the night. The Bible offers some good advice: "Let the evil of the day be sufficient thereof."

Several substantial studies indicate that our health depends not so much on the events that happen to us as on our reaction to them. In his fine book, *Who Gets Sick,* Dr. Blair Justice writes, "How we look at a stressful situation, the attitudes and beliefs we bring to a problem influences the chemical messages the brain sends to the body. If we see things as hopeless and decide to give up, that decision is dutifully conveyed by the brain to the body, which proceeds to carry out the order." There's a lot to be said for positive thinking! [28]

In an earlier chapter, we cited research indicating that the intake of aged garlic extract can reduce stress. Although garlic is by no means the whole story in coping with stress that brings on cardio-vascular disorders, it is a part that warrants serious consideration.

Chapter 5

Promising Answer to Cancer, Aging and Memory Loss

Ever since 1913 when the American Cancer Society was formed as an army to defeat cancer, cancer has been winning the war. In this age of rubber statistics when figures can be stretched in any direction that the stretcher desires, it seems we are making gains, but are we?

A prominent wholistic doctor told the writers the following.

"When I began practicing medicine almost 30 years ago, the odds were such that one out of every five persons would develop some form of cancer in a lifetime. Now the odds have shrunk to one in every three."

Whatever the statistics say, the Big "C" is far from being reduced to a small "c" or eliminated from the alphabet of devastating ailments, mainly because orthodox medical research primarily limits itself to pursuing improved surgery, radiation and chemotherapy. "Cut, burn and poison" techniques deal with already existing cancer, not with preventive measures, to win the nearly One Hundred Years' War on cancer.

Let's take a quick look at cancer, how it starts, and the best strategies for preventing it and coping with it.

Biochemists agree that cancer is a complicated, under-cover disorder that often takes 15 or more years to develop to a detectable level. Its process breaks down into three distinct stages: (1) initiation (the starting point); (2) promotion (gaining a foothold); and (3) progression (spreading).

Among many major initiating causes – environmental chemicals, viruses, and oxidation – are tobacco smoke, industrial pollutants, vehicle and aircraft exhaust fumes, impure drinking water, ionizing radiation, heavy metals – mainly lead and mercury – insecticides, herbicides and fungicides and certain food additives.

Early Discovery

It is ancient history that environmental chemicals can trigger cancer. Two hundred years ago, physicians puzzled as to why London's chimney sweepers suffered a far higher incidence of scrotal cancer than the average person. Then Harley Street surgeon Sir Percival Pott traced it to their daily exposure to chimney soot. [1]

Polycyclic hydrocarbons in chimney soot are well-documented causes of cancer in animals and bracketed in the same carcinogenic category as tobacco smoke that attacks lungs, skyrocketing the risk of lung cancer and emphysema.

In a previous chapter, we pointed out that garlic is noted for binding with toxic heavy metals such as cadmium, lead and mercury and discharging them from the body before they can become cancer triggers.

Cadmium, in tobacco smoke, industrial plant discharges, and in some city water supplies, depresses the immune system. Although leaded gasoline is long gone, lead still pervades soil, lakes, rivers and ends up in drinking water and food. Relative to the latter, lead arsenate remains a popular insect spray on fruit trees, some of which enters the fruit – and us. Mercury is Murder Incorporated, depositing itself on nerve junctions, blocking nerve function, causing paralysis and, in extreme cases, death. Sources? Amalgam fillings in teeth, mercury in dental offices and in firms using mercury in thermometers or electric light switches, and mercury-contaminated, large sea creatures: swordfish, sharks and marlins.

More Than a Suspect

Suspecting that mercury in amalgam fillings depresses immune function, leaving patients vulnerable to cancer and other devastating diseases, David W. Eggleston, D.D.S., then a clinical professor of dentistry at the University of Southern California with a private practice in Newport Beach, California, launched a 1983 research project to investigate his premise.

He enlisted test subjects who, for the benefit of mankind and possible benefit to themselves, would submit to having all amalgam fillings removed and replaced with non-toxic fillings. One of us, Jim Scheer, took part in the Eggleston study, offering blood samples for analysis, before the experiment and after removal of his amalgam fillings.

At the experiment's end, the number of Jim's T-lymphocyte cells, in ratio to total lymphocyte cells, rose more than 30 percent – an appreciable strengthening of his immune function. A few words about lymphocytes offer a frame of reference for fully appreciating this improvement.

White blood cells, called lymphocytes, are produced in lymph glands. Those that pass through and are conditioned by the thymus gland, the master gland of the immune system, become T-lymphocytes. These cells identify and label harmful substances such as cancer cells, so that macrophages and other white cells will recognize these enemies and attack them. As we accumulate birthdays, the thymus begins to shrink and reduce its production of hormones and the power to condition T-lymphocytes properly. This is one reason that so much cancer occurs later in life, and that autoimmune disorders are so prevalent then.

Undisclosed Alternatives

National and state dental associations have insisted for decades that mercury fillings are not harmful, despite the fact that nearly 100 studies show that this is untrue. Not long ago, the California legislature sharply rebuked the California Dental Association for not letting patients know that there are harmless alternatives to mercury fillings. Inasmuch as most California newspapers carried this story, more of the state's population knows about these alternatives. Some of the wire services, radio and TV networks and cable systems also featured this story, so the California legislature has performed a valuable service to the nation.

However, toxic minerals are not the only causes of cancer. A third major cancer initiator is radiation from medical and dental X-rays, from uranium mines, nuclear power plant explosions – even from these power plants' function — or fallout from nuclear bomb tests.

Conditioning for cancer also may come from many kinds of damaging free radicals. Breathed oxygen, needed for metabolizing food for energy and warmth, gives life and also takes it away, by creating free radicals. These molecular muggers, which are short one electron, wrest an electron from an adjacent molecule and turn it into a free radical that attacks a next-door molecule for its missing electron, starting a chain reaction of destruction.

Many sources generate free radicals: the sun's rays, X-rays, electrical appliances, smog, an estimated 10,000 environmental pollutants — including cigarette smoke — contaminated food, and impure drinking water — more than 3,000 food additives, all forms of emotional, mental and physical stress – grueling marathons and muscle-exhausting physical work – sickness, accidents, and even the normal body process of keeping hormones in proper ratio and balance.

Molecular biologist Dr. Bruce Ames, of the University of California, estimates that our cells take 10,000 free radical hits daily. "DNA repair enzymes efficiently remove most, but not all of the lesions formed," he writes. [2]

Bring on the Garlic

How to beat cancer, a relentless and merciless enemy?

One the best ways is through a regular intake of garlic. Sloan-Kettering cancer authorities, doctors John F. Pinto and Richard S. Rivlin write that at least 20 ingredients in garlic prevent cancer or cope with it in as many as three ways: (1) block tumors from developing from precursor cells; (2) prevent cancer from spreading to vulnerable target cells, and (3) delay or reverse malignancy. [3]

"A number of these basic mechanisms of garlic action have been described and further research may establish the most relevant of these mechanisms, and pave the way for human intervention trials with garlic derivatives involving not only cancer prevention, but also cancer control," they write. [4]

Drs. Zin-Zhou Lui and John Milner, at Pennsylvania State University, and Dr. Robert I-San Lin found that oral doses of aged garlic block the change of normal cells into cancer cells in rats injected with DMBA, an established tumor-causative. The researchers claim that aged garlic is much preferred over other forms of garlic because it is most effective for this purpose and safe. [5]

Opponent of Breast Cancer

Aged garlic extract also minimizes the development of tumor-induced breast cancer. How? A study by Harunobu Amagase, M.D., while at Pennsylvania State University, reveals that aged garlic extract and one of its main compounds, S-allyl cysteine, prevent the binding of a chemical carcinogen to the DNA of rats' breast cells. [6]

Not long ago, sensational results of a study directed by Dr. Milner excited the world of biochemists. Two different types of breast cancer induced in rats were inhibited by compounds in aged garlic extract. [7]

"Odorless garlic worked just as well as odorized products,"

stated Dr. Milner to the press media. "These results have profound implications for humans in terms of preventing potential tumor formation."

Cancer is caused by the binding of a carcinogen to the DNA (nucleic acid) in a normal cell, converting it into a cancer cell. In an animal study by Dr. Milner, aged garlic and a combination of aged garlic and the trace mineral selenium were pitted against this process. Animals fed the garlic extract showed 66 percent less binding of the cancer causative to the DNA than the control animals, which received no garlic. Adding selenium to the aged garlic brought about even more exciting results. There was almost perfect protection against cancer – 99 percent less binding than in the control animals. Without a doubt, aged garlic and selenium are a lethal preventive power. [8]

Excessive Intake of Omega-6

Many studies by biochemist Dr. Gerhard Schrauzer, professor emeritus at the University of California at San Diego, show that selenium on its own is one of the leading preventive forces against all forms of cancer. "Selenium deserves more attention and use in the prevention and treatment of various forms of cancer," he maintains. [9]

A word of caution about selenium. It is a trace mineral and should be used in trace amounts – no more than 200 micrograms daily— for greatest benefit. High levels of selenium can be toxic.

There's a misconception about the relationship of fat intake to breast cancer that Robert I-San Lin, Ph.D, an eminent authority in nutrition, metabolic diseases and genetic engineering, feels strongly should be corrected. One school of thought holds that fat intake has nothing to do with breast cancer. Another, led by Dr. San-Lin, feels that it does. [10]

Dr. I. San-Lin writes that, some years ago, Professor Walter

Willet, chairman of the nutrition department at Harvard University, addressed a meeting on polyunsaturated acids in Biloxi, Mississippi. Based on a study of 8,000 women, he told attending scientists that the amount of fat intake is not associated with the incidence of breast cancer.

Voicing opposition, Dr. I. San Lin stated that the study on which Willet's assertion was based offered inadequate statistics and defective methodology. However, going on the reputation of Dr. Willet and Harvard University, the media spread what Dr. San-Lin calls a myth. The study recognized the total amount of fat taken in but not the different amounts of various kinds of fats.

Invitation to Illness

The scientific/nutrition community, including government agencies, "have failed to comprehend the differences" in fatty acids when setting dietary guidelines for cancer prevention, claims Dr. I. San Lin.

"They often lump all types of fat together or classify them as saturated, monounsaturated and polyunsaturated fat. Such approaches can lead to inappropriate or erroneous dietary guidelines," he writes. [11]

Failure to distinguish between Omega-6 and Omega-3 fatty acids is one of the problems. Most authorities consider the excessive intake of Omega-6 fatty acids a nutritional disaster that invites every kind of sickness, saps energy and shortens the lifespan, citing it as a major cause for an increase in heart attacks, high blood pressure, strokes, rheumatoid arthritis, cancer, depressed immune function, emotional depression and difficulty in thinking and remembering.

What's the reason? From the 1960s into the 21st century, when people were – and are — urged to slash their intake of saturated fats and substitute unsaturated fats, no one seemed aware that certain unsaturated fats taken in large amounts could throw off the balance between essential fatty acids and cause depression of the immune system. (This, in turn, makes individuals more cancer-susceptible.)

So the most frequently eaten salad dressings, mayonnaise, margarines, and cooking oils were derived from corn, peanut, soy, safflower, sesame and sunflower seeds – all rich in Omega-6 and poor in Omega-3.

Impending Doom

Mary Clarke. Ph.D, of the department of Nutrition Education at Kansas State University, claims that this ratio between Omega-6 and Omega-3 was about one to one a half century ago. Today, it is a frightening 25 to one – even higher in breast milk of many pregnant women: 45 to one. [12]

Pertinent to all ailments due to immune system suppression — particularly breast cancer — excessive Omega-6 prevents Omega-3 from contributing full support to immunity. Every cell in the body and the immune system, as well, has a certain number of receptors for nutrients. Receptors on cells are limited, like seats on a bus. A rich intake of Omega-6 overwhelms the receptors, and there's little or no room on the bus for Omega-3. So all cells suffer a shortage of Omega-3 — especially significant in immune system cells that defend us against breast cancer, other cancers and various other disorders.

In maintaining that the **kind of fat** accented in the diet greatly influences the defense against cancer or lack of it, Dr. I San-Lin also makes the convincing case that excessive arachidonic acid, heavily present in land animal-derived food, contributes to immune suppression.

He recommends including more Omega-3 in the diet in the following foods — fish such as salmon, bluefish, herring, sardines, anchovies and turbo – as well as walnuts and walnut oil, flax seed and chia seed. Low-cost Omega-3 supplements, too, are available.

He doesn't advise cutting out meats, just eating them in moderation, and increasing the intake of Omega-3-and aged garlic. [13]

To understand the full significance of the need for a proper ratio of essential fatty acids ratio, it is important to know that Omega-6, Omega-3, and arachidonic acid are converted into prostaglandins, short-term controllers of body functions. Excessive arachidonic acid can be hazardous to the health. Derived mainly from animal foods, arachidonic acid can also come from latter stage body transformation of Omega-6 and promote the making of prostaglandins of the type 2 series that cause inflammation and platelet stickiness that contribute to abnormal blood clotting, hardening of the arteries, heart disease, strokes and cancer. Arachidonic acid is particularly needed by fetuses and infants for proper brain and eye development and, in **moderate** amounts for people of all ages.

About Prostaglandins

Omega-3 contributes to the synthesizing of the so-called favorable prostaglandins, the one and 3 series, that reduce inflammation, prevent platelet stickiness, improve blood flow and bolster immune function. [14]

Both garlic and onion oils block the enzymes lipoxygenase and cyclooxygenase and reduce or halt the production of prostaglandins 2, write herbologists Michael and Janet Weiner. [15]

The Weiners also claim that, "since many cancers are prostaglandin-dependent, this may explain why the allium oils (in garlic) have anti-tumor properties." [16]

Still another factor— weakness or damage to cellular DNA — leaves us vulnerable to cancer, says Dr. Milner. "Garlic seems to work as a detoxin and also performs somewhat of a repair process on damaged DNA," he discovered in one study. "Not only can garlic inhibit tumor formation, it also appears to inhibit growth of human tumor cells in culture," adds Eric Schaffer, research assistant for this study. [17]

Potent Against All Types

A review of 23 studies by biochemists at the University of North Carolina indicates that garlic may be helpful in preventing and in coping with most types of cancer: breast, colon, head and neck, lung and prostate. [18]

Dr. Benjamin Lau cites a study of 41,000 Iowa women showing that those who include garlic in their food most frequently have a two-fold reduction in risk of colon cancer. "In other words, garlic can prevent colon cancer," he writes. [19]

A garlic extract, diallyl sulfide (DS), scored a smashing victory in preventing animal cancer of the esophagus, a relatively common head and neck tumor. Three hours after their intake of DS, animals were given a powerful chemical known to cause esophageal cancer. **One hundred percent of them remained cancer-free.** [20]

Smokers Still in Danger

In the Iowa study, smoking and ex-smoking women who ate the most vegetables and fruits, garlic included, were less prone to develop lung cancer. However, a heavy intake of produce didn't protect those who continued smoking. [21]

Research in China and the Netherlands also shows a cancer-preventive effect of garlic for non-smokers or former smokers, but not for those who continue smoking. [22]

Like smoking, a diet high in animal fat contributes to various types of cancer – particularly prostate cancer, indicate Drs. Pinto-Rivlin, whose success in using aged garlic extract for dealing with prostate cancer was covered in detail in chapter one. These researchers report that the total fat intake, as well as total calorie intake from animal fat and red meat, contribute to prostate cancer development. Considering the prevalent super-high intake of linoleic acid (omega-6) in contrast with Omega-3, they state that some biochemists suggest that linoleic acid is the fatty acid responsible for generating prostate cancer. [23]

Garlic appears to lower the danger from stomach and bladder cancers, as well. Sharp evidence of protection comes from an epidemiological study conducted in Cangshan and Quixia counties of China. Cangshan residents eat 20 grams of garlic daily. That's almost an ounce. Those in Quixia county rarely eat it. People of Quixia county suffer 13 times as much stomach cancer as those in Cangshan county.

A Pertinent Study

Garlic authority Dr. Benjamin Lau comments that Cangshan residents had lower amounts of nitrites in their stomach juices. Nitrites and nitrates are notorious for initiating cancer. [24]

This study moved Dr. Lau to work with several urologists in comparing the effects of garlic on mouse bladder cancer with standard allopathic cancer drugs. Garlic worked significantly better! Dr. Lau then found that injections of garlic into mouse tumors brought about greater tumor shrinkage than the commonly used vaccine BCG. He writes that "after five treatments of garlic injected directly into the tumors, no cancer cells were present. Garlic actually cured the bladder cancer in mice." [25]

When garlic is injected into a tumor, immune system defenders immediately rush to the injection point, continues Dr. Lau. Other researchers, too, have noted that aged garlic extract attracts immune cells. [26]

Researchers Donald L. Lamm and Dale R. Riggs at West Virgnia University add an exciting footnote. "Of the many beneficial actions of garlic, inhibition of the growth of cancer is perhaps the most remarkable. Our previous animal studies demonstrated that aged garlic extract was highly effective and, unlike the approved immunotherapy for human bladder cancer, bacillus Calmette-Guerin (BCG), garlic was effective when added to the diet. Garlic can detoxify carcinogens by stimulation of enzymes, antioxidant activity and sulfur compound binding." [27]

A Versatile Defender

"Studies show a direct toxic effect of garlic to sarcoma, a highly malignant growth in connective tissue cells and gastric, colon, bladder and prostate cancer cells in tissue culture, but these effects cannot explain the inhibition of growth of transplanted cancer in animal models. The most likely explanation of this effect is immune stimulation," they write.

Drs. Lamm and Riggs indicate that aged garlic revs up the immune system by increasing its number of cellular warriors called lymphocytes and macrophages and their ability to infilter transplanted tumors, change them, stimulate the release of interleukin-2, tumor necrosis factor-a and interferon-y, and supercharge killer cells to attack tumors. Garlic appears to prevent suppression of the immune system that permits increased risk of malignancy. They conclude that "maintaining immune stimulation can significantly reduce the risk of cancer." [28]

Garlic also works in other ways to prevent cancer, state the West Virginia biochemists. It blocks the effects of malignancy-causing substances by stimulating anti-oxidant action of the enzymes of the cytochrome P450 family and by anti-cancer effects of garlic's sulfur ingredients. [29]

Veteran cancer researchers Judith G. Dausch, of the National Cancer Institute, and Daniel W. Nixon, of the American Cancer Society, believe that garlic intercepts cancer-causing agents on their way to cellular DNA. [30]

Various studies show that garlic can prevent skin cancers, one of the most prevalent kinds. Several research projects by Dr. Sidney Belman, of New York University Medical Center, reveal that topical application of garlic sulfides to the skin of mice prevented the development of tumors invariably induced by the carcinogen dimethyl benzathracene. [31]

For many decades, the Russians have used garlic for preventing lip cancer, based mainly on a successful experiment in 1958 by Drs. Sergiev and I. Leonov with 194 patients who had pre-cancerous white spots and hardened lips. They made a paste of raw garlic, generously smeared it on gauze, and then taped the gauze to the lips of the patients for from eight to 12 hours. After a single application, 184 of the 194 patients were healed. [32]

Authorities Are Convinced

Sold on aged garlic, Dr. Benjamin Lau reveals that research in his lab and that of others demonstrates that garlic can definitely block the formation of cancer-causatives and detoxify or eliminate them. Revving up the immune system – a key garlic function – is a paramount means of coping with all kinds of cancer, he maintains. [33]

Even conservative members of the biochemical research community accept the fact that garlic is a powerful weapon against cancer. For instance, William Blot, Ph.D., a biostatistician at the National Cancer Institute in Bethesda, Maryland states that "the weight of evidence is making it look like garlic really is protective against cancer. [34]

In an article in *Scientific American*, Dr. Eric Block, professor of chemistry at the State University of New York at Albany, one of the world's leading authorities on garlic, goes even further. He lists major nutritional and pharmacological contributions made by garlic: blocking cancer cell formation and spread and acting on enzymes that control cell division; reducing total serum cholesterol and low density lipoprotein (LDL) and raising high density lipoprotein, the good cholesterol; decreasing the tendency of blood to clot abnormally and to contribute to strokes and heart attacks; inhibiting inflammation by modulating arachidonic acid's conversion to the series 2 prostaglandins; guarding the liver from damage from chemical pollutants and drugs; annihilating intestinal parasites and harmful bacteria; acting as a shield to protect against damage from radiation, and, as an anti-oxidant, protecting sensitive cell walls from sabotage by free radicals. [35]

Revs Up Thinking and Remembering

Garlic is a major player in life extension, insist many biochemists. This is why Dr. Ronald Klatz, president of the American Longevity Institute in Chicago, repeatedly says the following to attendees at the organization's annual anti-aging conferences:

"Garlic is an extremely important healing and anti-aging food – one of the most perfect disease-fighting foods we have. I wish more medical experts would prescribe garlic to their patients to preserve the cardiovascular system, prevent disease and, of course, retard the aging process."

Dr. Klatz does exactly what he advocates. He takes eight capsules of Kyolic daily.

A much-taken-for-granted part of aging in many people is memory loss and slowed ability to think. Dr. Y.X. Zhang, a biochemist at the University of Tokyo, feels that this deterioration need not necessarily happen and can often be corrected. He accomplished this with mice. After speeding their aging and mouse-like senility by removing their thymus gland – the key gland of the immune system — Dr. Zhang fed the animals aged garlic extract and increased their thinking ability and memory for solving mazes. He theorizes that this upsurge to mental normality may be due to improvement of impaired immune function. [36]

Dr. San-Lin adds a postscript:

"Garlic enhances blood circulation to the brain, which helps prevent senility, Alzheimer's and even Parkinson's disease. I feel that garlic can target certain areas of the brain and enhance their performance – particularly in increased memory and performance." [37]

No Magic In Sexual Comebacks

Another failing ability with advancing age is taken for granted – sexual decline: inability of the male to develop or sustain an erection. Numerous animal studies suggest that aged garlic can help change this condition to some degree. Several alternative doctors cite specific cases in which aged garlic led to youthification of sexuality. However, as in all things, patients – and some physicians – seek the magic pill. Actually, this pill becomes more magical when patients work to improve their total body condition.

Couch potatoes must uproot themselves and take up to 30 minutes of aerobic exercise daily – with their doctor's approval of course – and enhance their diet, cutting down on refined carbohydrates and fats, sleeping better, reducing their weight and taking a positive attitude about their health. The latter helps enhance everything else they do.

Regular aerobic exercise helps to restore metabolic health in the penis, opening arteries for improved blood circulation, states physiologist Dr. C.A. Darby in the journal *Urology* (56: 302-306, 2000).

For ten years, Dr. Darby studied the relationship between erection difficulties and lifestyle in 1,000 Boston men. The two most important negative factors were lack of physical exercise and obesity. He suggests that a two mile walk five days per week could minimize or eliminate this problem that devastates many men and deprives them and their mates of sexual satisfaction.

Obesity ties right into under-exercising and over-eating as a deterrent to healthy erections. A paper presented at the American Urological Association Annual Meeting made the telling point that men with 42-inch waistlines had double the risk of developing erection problems as men with 32-inch waistlines. In addition, men who exercised for 30 minutes daily had the lowest risk of erectile dysfunction of all. [38]

Combine blood-circulation promoting aged garlic – the magic pill – with unmagic daily aerobic exercise and unmagic weight control and you have a winning formula!

Chapter 6

Super Natural Antibiotic

Thousands of years ago when Chinese, Egyptian and Greek doctors knew nothing about bacteria, viruses, fungi and yeasts, they cured diseases by trial and error, rejecting substances that didn't work and retaining those that did. Garlic, taken internally or applied externally, was one of the natural curatives that survived testing for many ailments and many centuries.

Scores of medical publications state that, since ancient times, Chinese doctors fed garlic to pneumonia and dysentery patients, administered garlic juice for typhoid fever and meningitis, and used garlic juice and its fumes to relieve colds, flu, sore throats and whooping cough symptoms.

Chinese doctor-researchers in 1950 sprayed garlic mist into the nasal passages of mice, later exposed to influenza virus, and prevented them from contracting this easily-spread disease.

Legend holds that, during the Black Plague in England, many people wearing necklaces of garlic avoided illness and death, and individuals living above a basement where banks of garlic were stored survived in good health.

Ever since word about the germ theory of disease become known worldwide, various cultures have used garlic as an antibiotic. During World War I, when there was more demand than supply of medicines, British army physicians wrapped wounds in garlic-soaked moss or bandages to prevent infections and healed them. During World War II, before medicinal antibiotics were available, Russians painted wounds of their soldiers with garlic juice and fed them garlic, too. In fact, garlic was nicknamed "Russian penicillin."

From Skeptic to Believer

In his information-packed book, *Garlic and You*, researcher Dr. Benjamin Lau admits having been a staunch skeptic about garlic's antibiotic value when a physician friend told him he had had remarkable success in treating a textbook full of ailments with this natural product. He mentioned that garlic is a powerful antibiotic and inhibitor of many bacteria, viruses, protozoa, fungi and parasites. [1]

Dr. Lau's first impression was "how can a successful, respected and well-published physician use folk remedies when an armament of modern medicine exists?" However, being a medical doctor, a professor of microbiology and an open-minded scientist, Dr. Lau decided to do some testing, introducing diluted garlic extract into several bacterial and fungal cultures and incubating them overnight.

Next morning the skeptic lost much of his skepticism. The garlic solution had abruptly stopped the growth of these cultures – more effectively than the most potent drugs then in use.

One of his Ph.D students pointed out many references by microbiologists reporting similar findings, indicating that garlic is "a potent, broad-spectrum antibiotic." Dr. Lau's remaining skepticism vanished like the growth in his garlic-treated cultures.

How does garlic cope with microorganisms?

One of Dr. Lau's students furnished an answer in an experiment that pitted garlic powder against the yeast organism Candida albicans. Garlic won by disabling the enzymes that form fats in the yeast cell membranes, making it impossible for them to take in oxygen. [2]

Next, one of Dr. Lau's graduate students divided two groups of mice infected with Candida albicans into two groups – one group receiving Kyolic aged garlic extract and the other (controls) receiving a saline solution. Within 24 hours, garlic had reduced the Candida colonies in the blood to just 400, compared with 3,500 by the saline solution, making it almost nine times more effective. Within 48 hours, garlic had annihilated **all** of the Candida colonies, compared with 1,400 still remaining in the saline-treated group. [3]

More Than an Antibiotic

The name "antibiotic" for garlic describes less than a half of its functions and power in coping with infection and disease. Garlic battles infectious agents directly and, also, indirectly through strengthening the immune system. Dr. Hirochi Sumiyoshi, of the University of Texas M.D. Anderson Cancer Center, says that aged garlic extract can be used along with conventional antibiotics, helping the body to fight off infection and boost the immune system. [4]

For more than 25 years, a stubborn and difficult-to-treat disease, viral encephalitis (inflammation of the brain) has been successfully managed with garlic by neurologists at the Shanghai Second Medical University in China. They claim that most viral encephalitis is started by the herpes simplex virus and that garlic is their choice substitute for conventional medicines for this condition. Aged garlic extract is free of side effects. [5]

Amebic dysentery, unceasing, severe, often bloody diarrhea, near epidemic in the United States in the early 1930s, before antibiotics were available, and widespread in primitive Africa, was a disease that, then, generally had to run its course. Medical missionary and Nobel Laureate Dr. Albert Schweitzer, famous for his humanitarianism and philosophical book, *Reverence for Life*, established a hospital in Lamborene, Gabon (then French Equatorial Africa). No conventional medicine was available to cope with this condition, and, to spare patients endless suffering, Dr. Schweitzer took a cue from European and Chinese folk medicine, and successfully treated thousands with garlic. [6]

Versatility Beyond Belief

Dr. Lau reports that a Tufts University medical student doing nutrition research at the Weismann Institude in Israel discovered that garlic stopped growth and spread of Entamocha histolytica, an organism that triggers some 400 million cases of dysentery throughout the world each year. The student learned about garlic's preventive and therapeutic powers from a Peace Corps volunteer at a time that no one at Tufts knew about garlic as a remedy. [7]

Numerous studies validate garlic's value in immobilizing protozoa such as toxoplasmas, cryptosporidia, and isopora. Most prevalent in cultures where sanitation practices are minimal, toxoplasmas are not uncommon in developed nations, transmitted by cats, dogs, mice, hens or ducks – the latter numerous in ponds and on shore in public parks. Toxoplasmas are banana-shaped protozoans that burrow into body cells and form cysts that contribute to symptoms similar to those of typhus or glandular fever. Although these organisms may be dormant tenants for years, they should be evicted as soon as detected, because they can contribute to various forms of heart disease and inflammation of the brain. [8]

Extremely toxic drugs are now being used to curb toxoplasmas, often with horrendous side effects, so aged garlic extract is worthy of consideration once a diagnosis for this condition has been established.

Devastating to Harmful Worms

Through the centuries, the Chinese have used garlic to kill various parasites that invade the body, causing illness or even death: hookworm, tapeworm, and trichina. Hookworms invade the intestinal tract of some individuals in the tropics or semi-tropics, rarely in more temperate lands. These parasites may cause enduring digestive upsets, strength-sapping anemia, and mental lethargy that apes difficulty in thinking and remembering in patients with low thyroid function.

As their name implies, tapeworms are flat and can grow to 15 to 20 feet long in animal or human intestines. Hooks on the side of their nobby heads attach themselves to the intestines, where they enjoy some of the host's digested food – a reason why some individuals with a lusty appetite are often asked if they have a tapeworm. Most tapeworms come from lightly cooked beef or fish.

Trichina, tiny worms in pork, can damage the intestine, and multiply into hungry hordes in this warm and moist environment, injuring the sensitive intestinal lining and causing fever, edema, muscle pain and shortness of breath like that associated with heart, lung or kidney disease.

From childhood, we are warned not to eat lightly cooked or "pink pork" and with good reason. Pigs are noted for hosting trichina and transmitting it to human beings. Cooks who fail to wash their hands and gripping utensils thoroughly after handling raw pork and fail to disinfect their kitchen counters where the meat has lain, place themselves and others in the home at risk of serious illness.

Chinese medical doctors are noted for recommending the intake of aged garlic extract to expel these intestinal worms – 600 milligrams three times daily.

Hazards of Conventional Treatment for Fungi

Many doctors dislike treating fungus infections – such as overgrowth of Candida albicans – because doses of allopathic medicines for such conditions need to be so high for so long that they can cause damaging side effects. Some conventional physicians, along with their holistic counterparts use aged garlic extract for these ailments with good results. [9]

Biochemists at the University of New Mexico School of Medicine tested garlic against fungus in test tubes and in animals and find it effective. Working with researchers at the Veterans Administration Medical Center in Albuquerque, they subjected several types of Crytoccocus neoformans to diluted, fresh, garlic juice and stopped its growth. This type of fungus starts an occasionally lethal form of meningitis, inflammation of the brain coverings.

Confirming the validity of these findings, researchers at China's Shanghai Second Medical University, told the First World Congress on Garlic that they had treated crytoccocal meningitis successfully for 30 years with garlic extract.

Powerful Immune Booster

Numerous studies show that garlic is a powerhouse immune stimulator.

Once the immune system detects an infection or pollutants in the body – cancer cells, as well — the reaction is like calling out the Marines in a military action – actually, more like also alerting the Air Force, Army and Navy and Coast Guard. The immune system's defense elements are B lymphocytes, T lymphocytes, phagocytes, killer cells and natural killer cells. B lymphocytes, made in the bone marrow, produce antibodies to challenge threats – mainly the most common infections. The remaining types of immune cells engage any other foreign invaders in direct hand-to-hand combat.

The ability of aged garlic extract to rev up the defensive strength of the immune system should not be overlooked by doctors and their patients!

Chapter 7

Multi-Purpose Health Booster

Over the babble of hundreds of voices in a Las Vegas hotel lobby, during a break at an anti-aging medical convention, the discussion of five holistic doctors standing in a corner stopped Jim Scheer as he was passing by.

It was a fascinating topic: the Desert Island theme. If you were marooned on a desert island and had to choose just one nutritional supplement to keep you in good health, what would that be?

The candidates ranged from garlic to chia seed to desiccated liver, wheat germ, brewer's yeast, blackstrap molasses, royal jelly, vitamin C, vitamin B-complex, and vitamin E. Jim lingered close enough and long enough to overhear the final and unanimous vote. It was for a special kind of garlic, Kyolic, odorless and aged, for many reasons: effectiveness and richness in vitamins, minerals, protective antioxidants, natural antibiotics, ability to stimulate and support the immune system, trigger gastric juices for better digestion, encourage the growth of friendly intestinal bacteria, and prevent pneumonia, typhus and tuberculosis, cardiovascular conditions and cancer.

One of the doctors said with a smile, "There's one condition in which odorless garlic would be a dismal failure. It won't repel vampires." Amid laughter, they concurred that this particular desert island was not located in Transylvania, so it would have no resident vampires.

Their Desert Island selection is a worthy one, because aged garlic contains an awesome roster of nutrients. A leading herbalist in alternative medicine, Michael A. Weiner, Ph.D writes that "garlic and onion contain over 75 different sulfur-containing compounds," as well as "the bioflavonoids, quercetin and cyanidin." [1]

Aged garlic includes them, as well as the following:18 amino acids, including every essential one, vitamins A, B-1, B-2, niacin, B-6, B-12, folic acid, C, and E; the minerals calcium, copper, iron, magnesium, potassium, selenium, sulfur – many forms – and zinc; as well as enzymes, flavonoids, fructans, nucleosides, saponins, sterols, and various other nutrients with health-promoting properties: fructosil arginine, carbolines, s-allyl cysteine and s-allyl mercaptocysteine.

Secrets of a Natural Healer

The charming book *Why George Should Eat Broccoli* by Paul A. Stitt lists 35 anti-cancer factors in garlic and onions.

Many holistic physicians use raw and Kyolic garlic for preventing and alleviating human illnesses. One of the most noted was the late Willem Khoe, M.D, Ph.D, who attained his medical degree at Loma Linda University and, for many decades, practiced in Las Vegas, Nevada. His fame was so widespread for successfully treating patients with natural foods and supplements — even for so-called incurable diseases — that sick people came to him from almost every continent.

Dr. Khoe referred to garlic as "God's gift to a toxic world" and stated that he used liquid aged garlic in his offices "for detoxification – especially for patients living in areas with much pollution and smog. Aside from treating patients with it for high blood pressure, cholesterol and triglycerides, as well as acute colds, diarrhea, and diabetes, Dr. Khoe recommended it for depression, patterning this use after that of a psychiatrist friend,

"A well-known psychiatrist who practices in Utah, uses liquid garlic in a remarkable way," he told two of the authors, whom he had known for many years. "He first used the garlic on himself to bring himself out of a severe depression, and, now, after 21 years of prescribing drugs to his patients for mental depression, he is giving them liquid garlic with vitamin B-1."

Dr. Khoe recommended various forms of Kyolic, aged and odorless garlic produced by Wakunaga of America in Mission Viejo, California for convincing reasons. It had been proved by hundreds of research projects – many of them double-blind — to bring positive results. Dr. Khoe told two of us about the common ailments for which he recommended aged garlic. Let's take them in alphabetical order.

ARTHRITIS – "First find the reason or reasons for this condition. Then have the patient keep his or her diet free from simple sugars and take six to eight 400 mg capsules of Kyolic daily. This modality relieved many of my patients of arthritic pain."

ATHEROSCLEROSIS and HEART DISEASE — Six to eight capsules of aged garlic daily.

ATHLETE'S FOOT — Apply plain, liquid Kyolic to affected areas with a Q-tip.

CANCER – "I did not use Kyolic directly for cancer treatment, although many studies show it to be helpful. Actually, I recommended it as an adjunct to cancer treatment, because it often reduces the burn side-effect of radiation. Kyolic brings most patients a feeling of well-being when used along with radiation or chemotherapy."

COLITIS (inflammation of the colon) – "I have relieved both acute and chronic colitis pain in my patients by having them take two teaspoons of liquid Kyolic daily and six capsules of Kyo-Dophilus (friendly bacteria) after each meal."

CONSTIPATION – "Kyolic has been extremely successful

in treating this ailment with four capsules daily before bedtime, along with 2 Kyo-Dophilus capsules after each meal."

DIABETES – "This disorder calls for a radical change of diet: no simple sugars – only complex carbohydrates, protein and limited fat. On this diet and 6 to 8 capsules of liquid Kyolic daily for several months, my patients were able to reduce insulin intake sharply and eventually eliminate it."

EAR INFECTIONS – "Carefully using a Q-tip, place 3 to 4 drops of liquid Kyolic in the ear canal. This helped patients to clear up bacterial and fungus infections of the ear canal."

GASTRITIS (inflammation of the stomach lining) – "First find the cause. If there's no malignancy, use two teaspoons of plain Kyolic liquid garlic and six Kyo-Dophilus capsules after each meal – a help for gastritis and even ulcer."

HAIR LOSS – "Use six to eight capsules of Kyolic daily to slow or stop excessive hair loss. In a number of cases, the hair growth has increased. Certain patients reported that some of their gray hair had reverted to its former color."

HYPERTENSION (high blood pressure) – "Two capsules of liquid Kyolic before each daily meal have controlled hypertension in numerous of my patients."

INFLUENZA (acute, infectious, virus disease) – "Many of my patients with early symptoms of flu have been relieved by taking 6 capsules of Kyolic garlic a day."

NASAL CONGESTION (also watery discharge) — "My patients have been helped by inhaling garlic vapor. They use 1-1/2 teaspoons of liquid Kyolic mixed with water in a vaporizer."

SINUS HEADACHES – "For this condition, here's what I

tell a patient. 'Sit erectly in a straight chair and hold your head back. Then squeeze three drops of aged garlic extract into each nostril. Wait for three minutes, then stand up, pinch your nostrils together, and blow out of your mouth four times, like putting out candles on a birthday cake. And it's gone! I recommend doing this ONLY for a sinus headache. I also suggest drinking at least 8 glasses of pure water and taking 3 to 4 capsules of Kyolic Formula 103 daily to prevent the onset of this condition."

SKIN LESIONS AND HEMORRHOIDS – "A few drops of liquid Kyolic on a Q-tip applied to skin sores, bites and insect stings – also abrasions – has speeded healing of my patients."

THROAT SORENESS – "My patients gargle 1/2 teaspoon of liquid Kyolic five times daily. This should be diluted in water for sore and infected throat, tonsillitis and laryngitis."

WORMS (pinworms) – "Advice to mothers of my child patients: Insert two capsules of liquid Kyolic into the rectum of the child before bedtime. Worms usually vanish within a few days."

Like Dr. Khoe and various other alternative medical doctors who give Five Star ratings to Wakunaga of America's aged garlic products, patients often report their unique experiences with them in letters to the firm's headquarters in Mission Viejo, California.

Here's a sampling of them in alphabetical order according to the medical ailment described. Some letters are condensed to conserve space. Initials of patients are used in most cases to protect identity and privacy.

ALLERGY

Even the smells of incoming mail would make me feel spacey and fatigued, so I had to hang letters on the clothesline for several days before bringing them into the house. I had a similar reaction to ink and couldn't write letters with ink. The smell of perfume caused me to pass out. This made it impossible for me to ride in a car or to be around people.

Then I started taking Kyolic liquid garlic formula 102 – ten capsules a day and 15 to 20 when under stress. It is working so well I can hardly believe it. I rode in a car for the first time in two years, and, during the Christmas holidays, visited with 11 people for seven and a half hours without getting sick. After my grandmother died, I was given some of her furniture, which had 60 years of cigarette smoke and heavy, oil-based perfume smells in the wood. In the past, I would have lapsed into semi-consciousness after a few whiffs. Now there's no problem. I can even write letters with ink. The change in me is truly wonderful.

L.C., Nevada

ALLERGY and RELATED CONDITIONS

I am an acupuncturist and was hospitalized twice for what was then an undiagnosed chemical toxicity from new carpeting in my office. My symptoms resembled those associated with a stroke: breathing problems, slurred speech, improperly selected words, stuttering and memory lapses.

Thanks to the suggestion of a colleague, I tried a Kyolic supplement called Neuro-Logic, a product based on aged garlic but also containing folic acid, Vitamin B-12, lecithin, ginkgo biloba, phosphatidylserine and acetyl L-Carnitine. My results were dramatic and immediate. In three days, I was experiencing just half of my problems. After four months on Neuro-Logic, I am amazingly better. Instead of having speech problems a dozen times in an hour, I sometimes experience them only twice a month. That's why I plan to use this product for the rest of my life.

Naturally, I began seeing opportunities to use Neuro Logic in my practice. It is very helpful for the post-menopausal patient with memory lapses. My husband is benefiting from a related Kyolic product: Cardio Logic, with a base of aged garlic and natural vitamin E, vitamin B-6, folic acid, vitamin B-12, L-carnitine, coenzyme Q-10 and lipoic acid.

Although he was experiencing a non-specific pain in the heart area, his cardiologist gave him a clean bill of health but nothing to relieve the condition. After five days on Cardio Logic, he reports that the pain has slowly abated.

W.B., Arizona

Editor's Note: The Cardio Logic formula was created by a prominent heart specialist: Arnold Fox, MD, of Los Angeles.

ALLERGY, EARACHES, COLDS AND RELATED AILMENTS

Allergies to grass, mold, pollen and foods that make him itch and scratch are major a part of my 6-1/2 year old son's health problems. However, there are also earaches, sore throats, strep infections and colds. His tonsils were so swollen that he could barely push a drinking straw between them and had trouble breathing and swallowing. Our pediatrician told us that his tonsils would have to be removed.

Antibiotics didn't help much, so, when the last bottle was finished, we began giving him three Kyolic tablets per day. We've seen a big change in him. He's still thin, but filling out. His face is pink. There are no black circles under his eyes anymore. He doesn't itch anymore, sleeps better and longer and eats better. The swollen tonsils have gone down, and his energy is up! He plays outside at all hours and no longer gets sick.

One Happy Mom, Denver

AMEBIASIS

Having had digestive problems for years, I was frightened to learn my diagnosis — asymptomatic amebiasis — infection with an organism that's difficult to kill and eventually causes serious problems. The only drug treatments for this disorder are all toxic. Flagyl, the most common, can cause cancer. Amebacquin can cause blindness, and arsenic – no comment. In short, all the drug treatments are poisons, which the doctors hope will kill the germs before they kill you.

In just one day on Flagyl, I was deathly ill. And a friend suggested I try Kyolic Formula 103 with vitamin C (ester C) and calcium ascorbate. Taking six capsules three times a day, I finished the bottle, and my test for amebiasis came out completely negative. I followed this with another bottle a month later. Three tests over a six month period were negative.

Kyolic may very well have saved my life. I'm sure travelers who visit the tropics, or those who pick up this bacterium from contaminated water or food will be happy to hear about Kyolic's amebicidal potential.

J.R.L., New Jersey

BLOOD CLOTTING (ABNORMAL)

For the past 30 years that we have operated Uchee Pines Institute, we have been recommending Kyolic products. We appreciate this form of garlic very much, and use it in place of warfarin for its anti-clotting properties and give it to patients for cardiovascular conditions and many kinds of infections, including Candida albicans.

We regularly start a patient with one to three teaspoons of liquid garlic three times a day and more in very severely symptomatic cases. It is our practice to keep the patient on liquid garlic for three to four weeks, then switch to the capsules, using two of them three times daily for two to three months, depending on the seriousness of the symptoms.

Over and above treating patients, we offer new lifestyle patterns that promote wellness and longevity and prevent illness. Odorless, aged garlic extract is an essential part of these patterns.

Cordially,

Agatha M. Thrash, MD, Preventive Medicine
Uchee Pines Institute
Seale, Alabama

BRONCHITIS

For the first eight years of her life, my daughter battled bronchitis, flu and various other infections and was in the doctor's office many times. Three years ago, I started her on Kyolic capsules, emptying the contents onto a spoon at night. Since then she hasn't been to a doctor. Two years ago, I increased her intake an additional teaspoon of the liquid extract, plus five capsules every night.

As a result, I have a pink cheeked, healthy, eleven-year old who can't remember what it's like to go to a doctor. We owe her good health to Wakunaga's Kyolic garlic. She loves her garlic and brings it to me every night before she goes to bed and becomes alarmed if the supply is getting low and reminds me with "Mom, you must order more of my garlic."

I know you take a special interest in the manner in which your garlic is grown and prepared, and I, as a parent, am grateful for that. It is worth every cent, and, because of what it has done for my little girl, I consider it the most important bottle in my vitamin cupboard and refrigerator. Thank you with all my heart.

From a concerned parent,
A.M.H., Nevada.

CANCER

Our son was diagnosed with "terminal cancer," when he was four. Ever since then, we have given him both Kyolic and KYO-Green daily. I wanted you to know that Andrew, now six years old, is doing great, and we wholeheartedly believe in your products. We are overwhelmingly happy to share our story of our son's positive turn-around from a cancer death sentence.

Thank you so very, very much.
D. & L.S., Minnesota

CANCER (Bladder)

I'm relaying a phone message from an 80-year old man who has had bladder cancer. It was in remission 15 years ago, when he started taking Kyolic Aged Garlic Extract (AGE) and KYO-Green, a powdered drink mix containing young barley and wheat grasses blended with fine chlorella, brown rice and fine kelp. He believes these products kept him from developing cancer again.

K.E.C., Toronto

CANCER (Breast)

It was a year and a month ago that I got the frightening phone call from home at 9:30 at night when I was still at work at a job I loved at Time magazine. Dad told me my mom's biopsy had come back positive. There were three cancerous tumors in her left breast. He said it wasn't an immediate death sentence, but the road ahead was rocky.

I couldn't help much 800 miles away and couldn't leave ev-

erything up to my Dad, so resigned my job, packed my bags, and moved back to the Midwest. Mom had always been an invincible women who never caught a cold or slept more than five hours a night, always cheerful, always active and on the go.

The oncologist said she required several surgeries and at least eight months of chemotherapy. Her hair started to fall out, her energy plunged to zero, her immune system was shot, she couldn't keep food down, and there was nothing we could do about it.

Most of the oncologists' predictions came true. After the surgeries and chemotherapy, this invincible woman seemed anything but that. Exhausted, she couldn't keep her eyes open for more than 20 minutes at a time. She was nauseated, scared and depressed, because there seemed no positive steps we could take to help her.

After continual disappointments, we felt an incredible excitement and relief when we found Wakunaga products, offering a natural and logical way to help her body's healing process and keep us all healthy. Mom began the whole regimen: Kyolic Aged Garlic Extract, aged garlic capsules with vitamins A, C, and E, Kyo-Dophilus, to implant friendly bacteria in her colon, and glasses full of Kyo-Green.

In a matter of days, we noticed a difference in her condition. It was as if her body had been kick-started, and she was ready to fight the battle. Instead of lying depressed in bed, she was again writing letters, on the phone with friends, and playing with our new dog in the backyard. Dietary upgrading and low impact exercise soon had her making new life priorities. Now she took long walks, smiling as big as ever and soon, she was back working 40 hours a week at her favorite job and taking time to enjoy her family, friends and community activities as she had before.

Our experience would not have been positive without help from Wakunaga products that made us take active positive steps toward my mother's healing. Now each of my family members has made a commitment to healthy living and has made Wakunaga an important part of our lives.

Thank you from the bottom of my heart.

B.W., Illinois

CANCER (Lung)

Earlier this year, my 88-year old mother had a build-up of fluid in her lung. Immediately after her medical doctor examined her, he rushed her to a hospital emergency room, where a liter of fluid was drawn from her right lung. Tests to determine the cause of the fluid led to exploratory surgery and a prognosis of lung cancer.

Mother was sent home with "six months to live," and the prospect of chemotherapy, radiation or both. After a family meeting, we decided on neither. Networking with friends led us to try alternatives: Kyo-Green, Kyolic liquid, Kyolic 102, Cardio Logic and Kyo-Dophilus.

After taking these products for two weeks, Mom claimed she felt "better than ever" and started eating. He energy increased and her pale complexion showed some color. A month later, Mom had a doctor's appointment. The doctor was pleased with the new x-rays compared with the prior ones. "I don't know what you're doing," he told her. "but, whatever it is, keep doing it."

A few months have passed, and Mom is walking every day, if weather permits, and insists on cooking her own meals. We went shopping the other day, and she went to church on Sunday. Recently, I offered to stay with her for two weeks, but after a week, she said she didn't need my help anymore, so I returned to New York.

Being a breast cancer survivor myself, I tried Kyolic products and must say, I feel like dancing. My Mom and I can never thank Wakunaga of America enough!

Sincerely,
G.K., New York

CANDIDA ALBICANS

A Louisiana woman wrote to thank me for helping her to regain her health. She had scored 277 on my yeast questionnaire. Here are excerpts from her message as to how she had overcome her Candida albicans problem:

"Kyolic, diet and various vitamins and herbal supplements that I found in your book all helped. I believe I didn't have to use Kyolic after the third bottle. My real breakthrough came after I eliminated sugar and other carbohydrates. I was weak with what I thought was the flu and noticed that I could breathe through my nose, that my body pain was gone, and the burning sensation in my lower back had completely disappeared.

"The quote in your book from Dr. Glasser was very important to me. 'It is the body, not radiation or drugs, that must destroy cancer cells, if the patient is to survive.'My mother had just been diagnosed with cancer, and this was personal to me. I knew all the remedies you gave were up to me, and it was my body that would destroy the Candida cells, using all these tools. All the true examples in your book inspired me to continue. Hopefully, my story can do the same for others."

Sincerely,
William G. Crook, MD
PO Box 3494
Jackson, Tennessee 38303

Editor's note: Dr. William G. Crook is author of the perennial best-selling book on defeating Candida albicans, *The Yeast Connection.* We recommend it highly!

CANDIDA ALBICANS

While I was working as a model in Atlanta in 1969, I was stricken with an agonizing pain in the bladder and back that sent me to the hospital. Tests were negative, but I was put on antibiotics for a bladder infection. This went on for eight years – pain, exams, antibiotics for bladder infection. One doctor said I had a high yeast count, but that it had no relation to my pain. That should have been a clue to me.

Six months later I was on antibiotics for a sinus infection, and when my pain refused to go away, I visited a doctor, who diagnosed me with interstitial cystitis and treated me each month with installation of a combination of steroids in my bladder. This was an excruciating and dreaded experience for me. The worst part of it was that there was little relief from bladder pain, and I gained unwanted weight – terrible for a model. I had to quit working and live with my parents.

I had been attending law school for several years as a new career. However, when I graduated, I was in too much pain to work and again moved in with my parents. Between my antibiotics and going on a sugar binge, I was in such pain and so disillusioned with conventional physicians that I went to a Naturopathic doctor, who examined me and found that I had an extremely high yeast account. "That is probably the source of your pain," he said.

Based on my research on yeast infection, I almost eliminated sugar and other refined carbohydrates and began taking Kyolic garlic. My doctor also found that I was highly allergic to wheat and dairy products, two of my favorites. I eliminated these foods, continued on my aged garlic and, miraculously, was healed.

Many, many thanks!
Susanna, Atlanta

Editor's Note: You won't believe this. She takes a half bottle of aged garlic extract daily – even if the label tells her the exact amount recommended. "This is my Security Blanket and its proves to be safe for me." She says.

CANDIDA ALBICANS

From the age of 19 to my present age of 35, I have suffered from Candida albicans. It all seemed to start when doctors gave me antibiotics for various infections. Then I was diagnosed with yeast overgrowth, which several doctors couldn't cure. I was told to eat a lot of yogurt. This seemed to help, but then the condition returned.

I was always sleepy, my memory started to go bad, my hearing was affected, I was nervous, had loose stools and a problem with my eyes that were so painful and dry that when a test was taken to measure tear production with a film of paper, it had to be peeled off. This condition persisted for two years, and no eye doctor could understand its cause. I thought it was an allergy to food and drink, so I avoided food and felt minor relief.

Desperate, I heard of Kyolic and took it daily. Soon I noticed that allergy-like symptoms started to bother me less and less. I started with liquid Kyolic and now empty two to three capsules of the powder into a tablespoon of water three times a day. Now I have energy every day and am far less sensitive to environmental allergens. I still have to improve on my diet – cut out sweets and refined carbohydrates – but my Candida albicans is going away.

Thank you,
A.F., Michigan

CEREBRAL PALSY

Delivered via emergency Caesarian at 32 weeks gestation, Alex was diagnosed as having hypotonic cerebral palsy. His specialist in Fort Lauderdale said he would be a happy one year old for the rest of his life and for us to take him home, love him, and when the time comes, look for group housing for him.

We never believed this. In February of this year, after reading many articles and books on cerebral palsy and autism, we started supplementing him with two teaspoons of Kyolic with B vitamin supplements, 1/2 teaspoon of Kyo-Green and one Kyo-Dophilus capsule daily.

After just a few weeks, we noticed remarkable changes in his attention and interaction. Prone to frequent colds, nasal congestion and ear infections, Alex was delivered from all of this, to our amazement. However, gingivitis developed, and we rubbed his gums with Kyolic twice daily, and that soon disappeared.

Alex now is eleven years old. Although he still can't talk, he works three computers, dresses himself and seems normal. Gratefully, we have our child back.

We (Alex's parents) are positive the changes are due to these supplements, so we started taking them, too, and Jill's hypoglycemia and acute colitis have normalized. Chuck, who suffered from sinus infections and frequent colds and upper respiratory infections, is free from them on the same regimen: two teaspoons of Kyolic daily, one teaspoon of Kyo-Green, and two Kyo-Dophilus capsules. We have both experienced more energy and stamina.

Thank a lot,
J. & C., Florida

CROHN'S DISEASE (REGIONAL ILEITIS)

I've been suffering from Crohn's disease since an early age. This is inflammation of the lower part of the small intestine. Despite surgery to correct the matter, I still suffer horrendous pain for three days out of every month. I couldn't believe that aged liquid garlic could solve my problem.

My wife, a registered nurse, thought I was losing my marbles by taking this garlic. However, it worked. I'm happy to tell you that life is now beautiful, and my recovery has convinced my wife to start taking Kyolic, too.

Praise the Lord and pass the garlic!
S.P., Santa Monica

COLDS

I would like to thank your company for introducing me to Kyolic. I have been giving it to my twins and quadruplets almost every day. I'm happy to tell you that it has really prevented colds and trips to the doctor.

My babies and I really appreciate it.

M.S.L., New Jersey

DEPRESSION

Always an upbeat, energetic, happy person, my 88-year old father suddenly went into severe depression and had no wish to go on living. Nothing that the family did seemed to help. Part of his discouragement came from being unable to walk in a straight line. He seemed to wobble.

None of the specialists we took him to had an answer. My stepson suggested we try the aged garlic-based Kyolic product called Gingko Biloba Plus, which widens arteries and stimulates the mind. This revives some elderly people, so we put dad on three capsules daily. After a few days, dad could feel a difference.

It is now three months later, and Gingko Biloba Plus has brought back his positive attitude, renewed energy and ability to walk without wobbling. My dad says, "It's a miracle." We agree. Gingko Biloba Plus gave my dad his life back again.

R.B., New Mexico

DIABETES

An insulin-dependent diabetic for four years, my 17-1/2 year old daughter, due to her age and lifestyle, found it hard to control her condition on one insulin injection daily. The diabetes specialist told her that if her high blood glucose level didn't come down, she would have to have an injection morning ***and*** *night.*

This upset her, because she's already a pin cushion and has followed a strict diet religiously. We mentioned this to our chemist (pharmacist), who suggested that she try plain garlic – one tablet in the morning and one at night. Her blood glucose readings came down and have stayed down, but then we had another problem. The dental school where she is training as a dental nurse said that she smells of garlic and would have to stop taking garlic or be thrown out of the school.

Upset but wanting to continue her studies, she stopped taking the garlic for two weeks, and her blood glucose readings again went up. It was suggested that she try the odorless and aged garlic extract. She did, her blood sugar level came down, and stays down, so all is beautiful now!

V.P., Australia

DRUG DEPENDENCY

Thank you for the supply of Kyolic Neuro Logic supplement you sent us for research with young men taking part in our study programs and seeking to overcome various kinds of substance abuse.

We have seen excellent results from this supplement, which has proved itself in several difficult cases, enabling the young men in question to liberate themselves completely from long-term drug dependency.

I am deeply grateful to you for your interest in our work and for the practical support and guidance you have provided.

Rabbi Avraham Greenbaum
The Azmara Institute - Jerusalem, Israel

EAR INFECTIONS

My two-year old twin girls have had lots of ear infections. Many antibiotics helped only once in a while. After giving them Kyolic by mouth, I saw an improvement with their ears and general health.

When they were sick, I gave them each a half teaspoon twice daily. When they were well, I gave them a squirt once a day. They like it so well that they go to the fridge and bring it to me to give to them.

S.L., Lakewood, NJ

EAR INFECTIONS

When my 10-year old son was just a few months old, he suffered constant ear infections. After his pediatrician tried a dozen antibiotics and failed, he removed my boy's tonsils, all to no avail. This made me research health articles and books. I found that people in Europe and in early America used garlic for colds and ear infections.

Fortunately, I found a holistic doctor who gave me some Kyolic to use on my boy when the Texas wind blew and his ears would get stopped up. I would put some on a Q-tip, and he would suck on it when he was six months old. Later I gave it to him in a spoon, and he has never had an ear infection since. Now he looks for it when I open the refrigerator door.

L.H., Texas

FATIGUE

Fatigue has been my problem. For the past three weeks, I have been taking one teaspoon of the liquid garlic mixed in water with 1 1/2 teaspoons of Kyo-Green daily, plus two capsules of aged garlic. Working up to two teaspoons of each, I also put myself on a mildly restricted yeast-mold and sugar-free diet.

I'm happy to report that I'm feeling stronger already. In fact, last week, I was out every single night at some social function, and, generally, if I even go out just two nights in a row, I'm exhausted. Now all my friends are trying Kyolic garlic and Kyo-Green, too!

G.M., Arizona

FATIGUE

My family members and I love Kyolic supplements. My mother who has been suffering from chronic fatigue used the liquid aged garlic enriched with B-1 and B-12 and reported the same energy boost that she had from B-12 shots.

Washington, DC

FIBROMYALGIA AND CHRONIC FATIGUE

All my life has been filled with health problems. I was just able to function as a wife, mother, grandmother, owner of a hair salon and helper in my husband's work. Things worsened when my husband came down with hepatitis C and was completely disabled and in constant pain. For decades conventional doctors couldn't diagnose my case, thought that I was a hypochondriac who just wanted to get medicated, and claimed that my illness "was all in my head."

Psychiatrists only added to my depression. I spent most of my days in a bed, in pain and in overwhelming fatigue, finally turning to alcohol. I wished I were dead! Finally, I was diagnosed with fibromyalgia and chronic fatigue. If I hadn't my beloved husband, my children and granddaughter and faith in God, I probably would have given up. My prayers and my husband's were answered in a wondrous way.

My sister-in-law introduced my husband and me to a man by phone. An almost miraculous thing happened. This man not only encouraged us, insisting that we would both heal, he sent us alternative literature, explained how we should change our eating habits and lifestyle and even sent us nutritional supplements, mostly aged garlic extract.

After a half year on this regimen, I feel like a new person. So does Bob. What a renewal! And we owe it all to the loving man directed to us due to our prayers.

S.J., Los Angeles

HALLUCINATIONS & VIOLENT BEHAVIOR

I'm a visiting nurse to an 86-year old patient who is diabetic, blind and subject to hallucinations with periodic violent behavior. He also was losing interest in his environment, talked little, and had spells of confusion. The doctors at the Veterans Administration hospital told his granddaughter that his brain cells were dying and that they couldn't do anything about it.

His granddaughter read a booklet about ginkgo that I gave her and she started giving him Ginkgo Biloba Plus three times a day. Within three months, there was a marked improvement in his behavior and alertness, and he seldom hallucinates now.

Yours truly,

V.G., Atlanta

HEARING IMPAIRMENT

My 10 year old son is deaf in his left ear and has fluctuating hearing in his right – mostly bad. I started him on one tablet of Kyolic daily, and now his hearing is 75 to 100 percent better. I am truly pleased. So please send me a catalog and price list of your available products.

S.R., Wyoming

HEPATITIS C

My story is almost unbelievable. Two years ago, I was the picture of health – a happy married Mr. Energy -- riding a bike almost everywhere, working out at the YMCA six days a week, managing a house for recovering alcoholics and addicts and holding another job, too.

Then, over several months, my health fell apart, and my symptoms demoralized me: aching joints, abdominal pain and such exhaustion that I couldn't walk up a flight of stairs, let along ride my bike and work out at the gym. I was physically forced to close down the recovery house. The diagnosis was hepatitis C. (My wife was sick, too.)

A year and a half of doctors, specialists and interferon treatment almost killed me – along with the bleak prediction that, at best, I had just five more years to live. My faith in God saved me. With all my options in the medical field exhausted, I turned to a Higher Power for help. It came from someone I didn't know, thanks to a phone introduction to him by my sister. This man was so caring, he sent me booklets on natural healing, recommended a change in my wife's and my lifestyle, including eating habits, and even sent me aged garlic extract.

We agreed to follow his recommendations. He said that, on this regimen, I would experience a marked recovery within a year.

He was wrong! It has taken me six months to be healthy again. The same is true of my wife. This is nothing short of a miracle. I thank God for the man who gave me a new life.

B.J., Los Angeles

HYPERCHOLESTEROLEMIA

Early this year, I saw a 45-year old woman patient with a severe yeast problem – almost unable to eat anything, lots of gas, bloating, discomfort, and poor digestion. She had tried everything for the yeast infection, including Nystatin, with minimal help. We told her to take liquid Kyolic, three teaspoonsful, three times daily and follow a sugar-free diet.

Three months later, she phoned to tell me that, within two weeks, her symptoms were all gone. Now the remarkable part. She also told me that she had had familial hypercholesterolemia – with a cholesterol reading around 350, in spite of being a total vegetarian.

Using a lot of oatbran and charcoal, she was able to reduce it to 305. After two months on Kyolic, she had her cholesterol checked just for interest. It had dropped to 220! She said it had not been that low in her adult life. She said Kyolic was definitely worth its price.

C.L.T, MD, Alabama

HYPERTENSION (High Blood Pressure)

Several years ago, with no forewarning, my blood pressure shot up really high. My doctor immediately put me on a diuretic that made me feel bad and dragged out. Still my doctor insisted I stay on it. Despite the medicine, I found my blood pressure fluctuating even if I were sitting watching TV. I could hardly drag myself out of bed in the morning.

Reading about the side effects of diuretics scared me into deciding there had to be a better way. So I went to a health food store and started asking questions and was given literature to read on garlic. That did it. I started taking aged garlic along with my blood pressure medicine. After about three weeks, I started skipping my blood pressure medicine every other day. Later, I started skipping more and more medicine – all the while monitoring my blood pressure.

After three months, I quit the medicine altogether, because my blood pressure had dropped and stabilized, and I felt so much better, I couldn't believe it. Several months later after my physical, my doctor said, "Everything looks good, and you look like you're feeling better."

"I am," I replied. "Thanks to garlic." He looked puzzled and just grinned. My only regret is that I didn't' know about Kyolic odorless garlic when I started on garlic. My wife complained about the offensive odor from the brands I took at first.

When my wife saw the transformation in my health and the fact that Kyolic was truly odorless, she started taking it. Then my health food store began stocking it regularly.

B.G.M., Mississippi

HYPERTENSION

Kyolic Super 101 Garlic capsules have been such a Godsend to me, I'm sure they can be to others. They've helped me in two incredible ways. (1) I'm a teacher. My heritage plus the stress on my job make my blood pressure run high. I was able to tolerate my physician's prescription medicine only a few days due to allergic reaction to it. Urged by my parents to eat fresh garlic to control my blood pressure, I ate it rarely because of its offensive odor.

One day at a health food store, I decided to try Kyolic – that was a year and a half ago – and my blood pressure is down. With Kyolic and watching my diet, I have kept my blood pressure under control. (2) An added benefit. Eight years ago, I started having al-

lergy attacks. (I'm allergic to grass, trees, dust, pollen, dander, chalk and many foods.) I received injections for my allergies for 6-1/2 years and couldn't function without them. I haven't taken a shot for well over a year, and Kyolic controls my allergies, too.

Hospital records can verify that a year and a half ago, my blood pressure was 200 over 120. Now it has dropped 60 to 80 points. The public needs this kind of information. Since I am black and a teacher, I think I can help you get this message across.

NGH, Baltimore

HYPERTENSION

Different combinations of medicine that my doctor gave me for high blood pressure made me so ill I had to stop taking them, so a friend who owned a health food store suggested that I try Kyolic Green Label Garlic capsules.

I did. Within two weeks, my blood pressure was normal, my energy returned, and I felt great. When I told my doctor what had happened, he tested my blood pressure five times and finally believed the results. Inasmuch as he was on medicine for high blood pressure also, I treated him to a bottle of Kyolic. His results were the same as mine, and now the doctor swears by Kyolic garlic. Kyolic garlic saved my life!

G.C., California

HYPERTENSION

Until recently my husband had taken Regroton, a high blood pressure medication for nine years with the understanding that he would have to take it for the rest of his life. Regroton brought on complications. As a diuretic, it caused him to make middle of the night trips to the bathroom. Diuretics such as this remove minerals from a person's system, so he had to take nine potassium tablets a day and be tested twice yearly for blood potassium levels.

Then we heard about aged garlic, and my husband tried Kyolic Super Formula 100 – four capsules a day. From the very beginning, his blood pressure read the same with garlic as with Regroton. Our experiment was a whopping success without the complications of the prescription drug.

It's miraculous. No doubt medical doctors would pooh-pooh anything so simple, but they can scoff all they want. My husband is living proof that aged garlic works.

Thanks a million!
D.B., Oregon

IMMUNE SYSTEM WEAKNESS

Eighteen years ago, I weighed just 77 pounds, and, according to four different specialists, was dying right before their eyes. My immune system was so weak, I couldn't hold my own. At that time I turned to natural care. I couldn't hold up under the stresses of therapy and day to day living without Kyolic liquid garlic, Kyo-Dophilus, Kyo-Green, exercise and natural food.

When I started taking Kyolic and Kyo-Dophilus and minimized sugar to seven percent of my diet, I began to improve. I am far better, am able to eat many things I could not eat before, have gained weight to my normal level and have much more energy than before. Without Kyolic, I could not go on!

K.F., Canada

LIVER AND BLADDER DISEASE

Some months ago, an eminent professor and researcher of a southern university recently wrote you for samples of aged garlic extract enriched with vitamins B-1 and B-2 to try prior to his using them for research. He is a world authority on liver and bladder disease. I'm glad you supplied him with them, because, after trying aged garlic extract for a while, he has almost eliminated the need for drugs for his high blood pressure condition and believes that it can be helpful for liver and bladder disorders. Through his powerful influence, many other leading researchers will begin to use aged garlic extract in their studies.

L.B., Louisiana

MONONUCLEOSIS

An 18 year old male came to our offices with a 104 fever, positive Epstein-Barr (EB) virus (mononucleosis), very swollen and congested anterior cervical lymph glands, tonsils and throat swollen almost enough to occlude the airway, and an extreme overgrowth of black and green fungus covering the entire nasopharynx and tongue.

After appropriate chiropractic manipulations to appropriate areas, I put him on an improved nutritional regimen with the main supplement aged garlic extract. He took six capsules per day. In addition, I had him take two enemas daily for three days, then one a day, with one coffee enema also to complete the week.

Within that time, his body was clear of observable fungus. The fever and swelling of the lymph glands were also gone. Two weeks later, the E-B test ran nearly normal. Even though I treated this condition with a variety of items, I feel the garlic made the rapid difference.

J.D., Doctor of Chiropractic, Texas

PAIN AND DEPRESSION

As a pain reliever, I've met with success with both professional athletes – New York Giants, Rangers, Arrows, Nets, Knicks and Yankees and Olympians, as well as myself as a competing powerlifter. I've found that when Kyolic is taken after workouts/contests/games, it seems to prevent edema and the build-up of lactic acids in the cooling down muscles.

In weight-lifting, it has been particularly effective in helping us to "make weight" for our respective class. It seems to act in two capacities: as a mild diuretic and as an aid in breaking down fats and flushing them out of the body.

Lastly, and perhaps most importantly, it bolsters the immune system to fortify it against all stress of the competition/life. I have been an ardent user of aged garlic extract since its inception, because I remember the days before it when we were forced to use those inferior odoriferous capsules or the cloves themselves.

The toll of ingesting these was high socially and internally – as some individuals' systems react poorly to raw garlic contact. Thus, only a few of us brave souls dared prescribe it to patients, much less consume it ourselves. I am disturbed by the attempts of lesser product lines to defame your products. Thank God for your development of Kyolic. Keep up the great production. If I can assist you in any way, feel free to call.

Dr. R.M., New York State

SINUSITIS/ALLERGIES

I began using Afrim nose spray 20 years ago and was addicted until four years ago, when I moved to Palm Springs in the desert. I was constantly at the doctor for breathing problems, sinusitis, and allergies. This physician got me off Afrim to Nasalcrom nose drops and then to Nasalcort, a puff in each nostril once a day.

He told me I would have to be on this kind of medication for the rest of my life. It was only after I started taking aged garlic extract – two capsules daily — just a few weeks ago that I started feeling good again. For the first time in 20 years, I can breathe without a doctor's prescription. I just can't believe it is helping my respiratory problems.

I like to help others and that is the reason I wrote this letter. Hopefully, you will share it with others, and they will be helped, too.

S.K., Palm Springs, CA

STOMACH PAIN AND HIGH CHOLESTEROL

Fifty years old, I have been treated for more than 20 years by a succession of doctors for incessant stomach pain that almost drove me up a wall. Supposedly, there was an ulcer in my upper GI tract.

On top of that, I was told my cholesterol was too high and put on medication that cost $60.00 a bottle. It did little for my cholesterol, but it made me sick. Tired of it all, I took matters into my own hands and bought aged garlic extract, taking 10 capsules daily after meals to lower my cholesterol. Immediately, I started feeling better, and my stomach no longer pained me. For years, I couldn't eat an onion without feeling my stomach was killing me. Now I can eat and drink anything I like, and there's not a hint of a pain. My recovery has made a believer of my doctor who started taking Kyolic.

Thank God and Kyolic.

J.N., Kentucky

STROKE

Several years ago, tragedy struck in my life – a brain stem stroke, caused when blood thickens and can't pass through capillaries, forming a clot that cuts off oxygen to the area. I was paralyzed on my right side, lost my equilibrium, and was unable to walk. After release from the intensive care unit, I wondered "What do I do now?"

A friend answered that question, suggesting that I take Gingko Biloba Plus a combination of aged garlic extract, Siberian ginseng extract and ginkgo biloba leaf extract to supply more blood to my brain. Immediately, I started taking six capsules daily – two each morning, noon, and night.

After three weeks on this regimen, results were unbelievable. Most of my paralysis was gone, I had regained my equilibrium and was able to walk without assistance. My neurologist was amazed at my short recovery time, and told me that, in 20 years of practice, he had never seen anyone recover so fast from the type of stroke I had.

I shall be forever grateful to Wakunaga of America and all the people who helped them develop such a fine supplement as Gingko Biloba Plus.

M.H., California

TUBERCULOSIS and LUPUS

Having been diagnosed with tuberculosis five years ago, I was placed on a three drug therapy program for 19 months. This brought on extreme fatigue and fever, joint pain on my left side and up and down my spine, headaches, severe depression and sensitivity to the sun.

Within six months, I was diagnosed with lupus, asked to begin a new two-drug therapy and accept my disability and, therefore, inability to work. Instead of starting another toxic drug therapy pro-

gram, I began treatment with a homeopathic physician. He put me on a healthful diet, various vitamins and herbs and daily liquid Kyolic to detoxify. To speed up the detoxification, I put myself on periodic juice fasts with liquid aged garlic extract. Slowly symptoms began to disappear. Within the first year, my temperature normalized, 90 percent of my pain in the joints was gone, and I have no problems with the sun.

Blood tests still show that I am slightly positive to lupus. However, I am feeling so much better. Aged garlic extract is still very much a part of my daily life, and I am very grateful for Kyolic products.

A.L., Los Angeles, CA

ULCERS OF THE MOUTH

Since childhood, I have endured the painful and frustrating problem of chronic mouth ulcers. No doctor seemed to know what caused them or what to prescribe for them. Finally, my pain became so intense that I almost had to stop eating. The ulcers only got worse when my doctor put me on Zovirax, an anti-viral used to treat herpes.

Then I saw your ad for Kyo-Dophilus and decided to take two capsules an hour after eating, as directed. I took a two weeks trip, and, due to its rigors, was able to take only one capsule daily.

Miraculously, I have not had a mouth ulcer in four weeks, so I plan to continue taking the capsules exclusively. Most of all, I look forward to telling my physician that he now has an answer for other patients with this problem. In fact, I plan to sing your praises to everyone who will listen!

B.H., Alabama

P.S. Maybe some of your readers are not familiar with Kyo-Dophilus, so let me explain that it's a pro-biotic derived from human sources and brings an army of friendly bacteria into your system. It doesn't need refrigeration and has a shelf life of three years.

B.H.

Chapter 8

Exciting News from the Pet Set

Everybody knows that dogs can speak. Everybody also knows that they can't write letters. Neither can cats and other pets. Fortunately their masters and mistresses can and do. Some of their letters tell amazing stories about turn-arounds in their pets' health – particularly due to aged garlic.

THE FLEAS HAVE FLED

I have taken Kyolic aged and odorless garlic for three years and swear by it. I started giving my dog a capsule daily, too, and what do you know? He's flea-free. What's more, he doesn't smell of garlic.

M.J., Springfield, Ohio

MORE ABOUT FLED FLEAS

My first experience with the wonders of garlic and animals came when I first moved to Florida. "Oh, you don't want to have pets in Florida," well-meaning friends told me. "There's an awful flea problem."

However, I'd read that giving garlic to pets of all kinds helps them repel fleas, so from day one, I squirted aged and liquid Kyolic garlic on my pets' food. Well, now it has been 15 years and six pets later, and I've yet to see a flea on any of my pets.

L.A., Florida

I give my cats Kyolic every day for their general health, and they have never gotten fleas.

C.W., California

I've had my cat for two years, and she was infested with fleas until I gave her Kyolic every day.

C.P., Boston

My two Keeshond dogs are usually flea-infested every summer. However, since I have given them three capsules a day of Kyolic aged garlic extract, they have not had a flea on them, my groomer tells me. This is really exciting, because my dogs are allergic to anti-flea medications.

J.W., California

OF FLEAS, A CELEBRITY AND A CAUSE

Let me tell you the inside story about dogs and June Lockhart, who starred in TV's Lassie series some years ago. June is the celebrity spokesperson for International Hearing Dog, Inc., a non-profit organization that trains and supplies dogs to help people who are totally hearing impaired.

No solution or shampoo could help June get rid of her dog Tony's fleas. Someone urged her to buy a bottle of aged garlic extract and mix it with her pet's meals. Fleas simply disappeared.

A cause closest to June's heart is the International Hearing Dog, Inc., of Henderson, Colorado. "It's a wonderful program," she states. "Everybody wins. The deaf have a companion, and dogs — mainly small, mixed-breed and sensitive — are taken from animal shelters, where there's always a danger that they will be put to sleep."

Selected for friendliness, intelligence, adaptability, and eagerness to please, the dogs are trained for three months to respond to household sounds: a crying baby, a doorbell, an alarm clock, a smoke alarm, a security buzzer, or an intruder.

A trainer accompanies each dog placed with a deaf person and stays there a week to make sure that the person and animal work well together. Volunteers check periodically to see how the arrangement is working. If the person and dog are still compatible after a year, the dog is certified for that home.

Satisfied with how well aged garlic had rid her dog of fleas, June got in touch with Wakunaga of America in Mission Viejo, California, the producer of Kyolic. Would the company donate aged garlic extract to hearing impaired people with every dog trained by International Hearing Dog, Inc.?

They would and did. Congratulations, Wakunaga of America!

J.S., California

Editor's Note: Charlie Fox phoned June Lockhart and, in the process, asked her if she's taking odorless, aged garlic. "No," she replied. "I don't have fleas." After Charlie mentioned that fleas were not mandatory for taking Kyolic, June said she was going to try it, because Tony had experienced so many unexpected benefits from it.

EASING QUEASINESS

It all began when I started taking liquid Kyolic with vitamin B-1 for my queasiness. The cap of the bottle must have been loose, because when I opened the refrigerator door, the bottle fell to the floor and spilled. As I reached up for a paper towel, my puppy dog Buddy began lapping it up.

Occasionally I began to add a few drops of Kyolic to his food. Now when his stomach is upset and I'm taking Kyolic, he brings over his bowl. Its as if he knows that Kyolic will ease his queasiness.

C. & B.K., Miami

RED AND INFLAMED EYES

Mary is an herbal dog, so I sought an herbal solution when her eyes became red and inflamed: 25 to 50 drops of Kyolic liquid garlic mixed into an ounce of distilled water, applied with an eye-dropper one to four times daily.

I don't like playing around with eyes, so I made an appointment with my vet for 4:40 that afternoon. However, by 4:00 o'clock, Mary's eyes looked so well that I almost canceled the appointment. Then I decided to go anyhow to confirm or reject my diagnosis of conjunctivitis.

One look, and the vet said, "She's got conjunctivitis all right, but it's almost cleared up. What have you done?" He refused to acknowledge that garlic had helped. He doesn't believe in herbals and tried to sell me prescription eye drops containing cortisone for $46. I didn't buy.

Kyolic liquid really works. Some bacterial infection was troubling Gloria, my other dog, so I gave her a few drops. I put some of the same drops that were effective for Mary in my own eyes. What a lovely refreshing feeling! My husband tried some on his tired eyes and was quite surprised at the results.

In Kyolic health,
R.L., Mary and Gloria, Utah

DANGER OF CAT'S TAIL AMPUTATION

My cat Calico got hit by a car, and her hind legs and tail were injured. The tail was so bad — no nerve endings left – that the vet feared he might have to amputate it. He said that her back legs would not be paralyzed, but that it would take months for them and their bones to heal properly.

I couldn't stand the thought of Calico losing her tail, so I started giving her a quarter of a teaspoon of aged garlic with B vitamins once a day. She had a follow-up appointment with the vet a week and a half later, and he was surprised that Calico's tail had regained its proper nerve function. I was relieved and happy that this tale about my cat's tail has a happy ending!

N.E., California

CAT'S DEATH SENTENCE REVERSED

Pervis, my gray and white cat was weak, losing weight and diagnosed by the vet with feline infectious peritonitis. The vet suggested she be put to sleep. Instead, I gave her Kyolic aged, liquid garlic extract – five milliliters every two hours, five times daily.

Four weeks later, she had regained her weight, energy and was playing with other cats. After six weeks, I took her back to the vet, who was amazed. He had never seen a cat survive this disease!

R.L., Arizona

SORES THAT WOULDN'T HEAL

My beloved and wonderful Labrador Jesse broke out in nasty sores – I call them hot spots – on his back. I bathed the raw areas and applied triple antibiotic cream on them. Tortured by the itch, Jesse managed to scratch it off before a solid scar could form. Actu-

ally the hot spots started to spread.

I happened to be researching the healing power of garlic during this time, and came across a testimonial from a pet owner who had applied liquid garlic and healed a pet's wound. In desperation, I applied Kyolic to his sores, and, to my utter amazement the wounds almost healed by the next day. Jesse no longer itched, so the sores healed quickly.

L.A., Florida

MORE ABOUT UNHEALING SORES

After my Labrador Jesse's quick healing from sores on his back, I met an older woman when I was walking my dogs. Her boxer Buster had sores and bumps all over his back, and she was worried about his health. Nothing that the vet had suggested worked – swallowed or topical medication and a change of diet.

Based on my success with Jesse, I encouraged her to add Kyolic to Buster's food. She agreed to try it. It was several months before I saw her and Buster again. His "Mom" was ecstatic.

"Look at Buster's skin," she exclaimed. Sure enough, Buster's skin was silky smooth – not a blemish in sight, and his fur was glossy.

L.A., Florida

GARLIC VS. A VIRUS THAT ATTACKS HORSES

Symptoms of a virus that attacks horses are fever, coughing, mucus running from nostrils, fatigue, poor appetite and general disability. A bottle of aged and liquid garlic given on two successive days to each animal does the job of curing. One of my race horses developed the virus symptoms and was scratched from the racing program for the following day. I gave one bottle of liquid garlic to the animal, and he improved sufficiently to enter the race. He hit the board first, second, and third.

In another instance, the virus was running rampant in the bodies of Marty's Winter and Candy Mistico, so I gave them each two bottles of liquid aged garlic extract. They went on to race the next day, and both finished in the money.

A two year-old colt named Victor was in such poor shape, I didn't expect him to develop into a race horse. After taking liquid garlic over a brief period, Victor began feeling better and eating a lot more. He is now qualified to take part in any races in which he is entered. As a stable owner, I have to admit that taking aged garlic extract to the races pays off.

Clarissa McCord
Cavendish Stables
Cloverdale, British Columbia

COPING WITH KENNEL COUGH

Sometimes pets pick up various ailments when temporarily placed in a kennel with others. My little dog Bananas came down with a bad case of kennel cough, an ailment that can lead to pneumonia, so I started giving her twice as much Kyolic liquid garlic as usual – 12 drops daily, instead of six. Vets usually treat this with antibiotics and steroids, and it takes at least four or five days to go away. However, with Kyolic, her kennel cough went away in 24 hours.

Thanks a lot,

C.I., Utah

UPPER RESPIRATORY INFECTION AND BRUTUS

At first, I thought the sneezing of my 13-year old Siamese cat, Brutus, was an allergy that would pass. After a week, he began to wheeze and cough, so I brought him to a veterinarian, who thought his condition was an upper respiratory infection and prescribed an antibiotic. However, he didn't get any better, so I brought him back to the vet, who shook his head and said, "I can't figure this one out!"

I couldn't get a diagnosis out of him, and Brutus was now in agony, so I took him to another vet. He felt that Brutus was suffering from a chemical allergy, so we removed all perfumed room scents and changed to scent-free litter. Yet he still coughed and wheezed on occasion, his throat was irritated and sore, and he had lost his appetite.

The vet said he didn't want to use steroids that might be helpful, because of Brutus' age. I wanted to try herbal remedies, but he said not to mess with herbs, since some are poisonous to cats.

When I asked about garlic, he said, "Fine." Each day, I squirted several drops of liquid Kyolic into his mouth to reduce his throat irritation and build up his immunity. Soon his appetite increased, he regained his five lost pounds, and his cough was greatly reduced.

L.A., Florida

GARLIC VS. BOWEL BACTERIA

One of my three-pound Pomeranians picked up a bowel bacterium or virus that brought on diarrhea. Small animals can become dehydrated easily and seriously ill, so I had to nurse her around the clock, feeding her water by eye dropper. Usually a three-pound Pom doesn't survive after three days of diarrhea and dehydration. Nothing seemed to control her diarrhea, so I emptied the contents of two Kyo-Dophilus capsules on a bit of baby food and somehow got it into her. She didn't seem to mind the taste.

I continued the same dose of Kyo-Dophilus for a week, and each day she improved. I believe your fine product saved my Pom's life. I also persuaded one of our top breeders to use Kyo-Dophilus when she got some of her "girls" back from another kennel. They were all diagnosed with staph and had to take antibiotics. Thanks for Kyo-Dophilus, they suffered no ill effects from the antibiotics, and to this day, are all fine and producing.

I really believe in your good products and hope to educate our Pom club members even more so in order that their pets may reap the health benefits, too.

In gratitude and Pom love,

T.D., Utah

KYOLIC: A LIFE-SAVER FOR A CAT AND A MARRIAGE

Kyolic saved the life of my 14-year old calico kitty Amber, who also has beautiful amber colored eyes, as well as a marriage. The marriage is mine.

Trouble started when my husband, I and Amber moved from Arizona, where she was an outdoor cat, to California to a small apartment. The abrupt change of environment was a shock to Amber, and she didn't handle it well. She stopped washing herself regularly, and her coat became greasy and wouldn't lie flat.

Normally affectionate and mellow, Amber suddenly became whiny and mean. For no reason at all, she would howl in the middle of the night, keeping us awake, scratch on our bedroom door, trying to get in, and bite our legs when we walked close to her. Amber was miserable and stopped eating. We were getting stressed out, too – especially my husband.

The straw that broke the camel's back was when she started to poop in the shower and my husband's study. My husband, who is nearsighted, wakes up before me and showers. Unfortunately he discovered one of Amber's mistakes with his foot. Then came the ultimatum. Either Amber behaves, or we get rid of her!

In desperation, I tried everything, giving her more attention – but she refused to be held – gave her the best quality canned cat food, which she ate, but now she increased the frequency of her mistakes – not only in the shower and study, but all over the house.

"She's so senile she should be put away," insisted my husband. It boiled down to that either Amber or he would have to go.

A veterinarian diagnosed Amber's condition as stress and suggested giving her Kyolic. After I squirted a teaspoon of Kyolic on her saucer of food twice daily for a few days, she ate markedly better, she started washing herself again, her disposition shifted back to affectionate and mellow and her mistakes stopped. After half the bottle was gone, she was the old Amber again. When I held her, I noticed that her fur head had become incredibly soft, just like that of a bunny rabbit.

Thanks to Kyolic, the crisis is over, and we are again a happy trio. Kyolic works to relieve stress for man or beast. Thank you, Kyolic for saving my cat and marriage!

K.M., California

A VET'S ADVICE ON HEALING PETS WITH GARLIC

(Editor's Note: Gloria Dodd, DVM, of Gualala, California, with many decades of practice, offers you a career's worth of successful experience in treating pets with garlic. Her recommendations are not limited to just dogs and cats, but also cover horses and birds. These include proper dosages for small, medium, and large dogs and cats – as well as horses and birds.)

Throughout my practice, I have frequently used Kyolic liquid successfully in treating sick animals, as well as for maintaining and promoting their good health. Kyolic liquid is a safe and effective treatment for animals, which enables poisonous substances to be eliminated naturally. The constituents in aged garlic extract, mainly the sulfur-containing compounds, have an affinity for attracting toxins within the stomach and intestines and enhance their excretion from the body.

Effective against fleas, ticks and other parasites, aged garlic is excellent for maintaining and promoting the general health of animals, strengthens their immune system, helps the body eliminate toxins, invigorates the animals, and improves the quality of their coat.

In our valley, many dogs were dying of acute toxemia (poisoned blood) from a parvo epidemic, and their percentage of mortality was running very high when they were treated only with standard/orthodox therapies. When liquid garlic was added, along with a total treatment regimen, I was able successfully to treat parvo virus, a new strain of virus in dogs that causes severe hemorrhagic gastroenteritis and death. I was able to save many of my parvo dogs.

For dogs and cats, Kyolic liquid may be used as a supplement for detoxifying, for the treatment of other virus infections and various other health disorders, including indigestion, pancreatic and liver problems, diarrhea, other health conditions, and is always the treatment of choice for dermatitis (skin inflammation), no matter what the cause.

For these purposes, for small cats and toy breeds, I administered 1/2 teaspoon of aged liquid garlic three times a day for one week and 1/2 teaspoon once a day thereafter for maintenance of health. For medium size dogs and cats, the dosage should be increased to one teaspoon three times a day for a week and one teaspoon a day thereafter for maintenance of health. For large dogs, one tablespoon three times a day for one week, and one tablespoon a day thereafter for maintenance of health.

The success of aged garlic is not limited to small animals. Other veterinarians report other excellent results when using it to treat horses which have virus-related symptoms such as fever, coughing, fatigue, excess mucus in nostrils, and general disabling conditions. In these cases, one bottle of liquid Kyolic (2 oz.) was given at feeding time for two days. It is best to mix the Kyolic into their food such as alfalfa.

Other veterinarians successfully use aged garlic liquid for treating their birds which have candidiasis and related illnesses. One and a half teaspoons should be mixed in their water daily until symptoms are gone.

In my opinion, every illness is an accumulation of toxins within the body, be it of bacterial, viral or chemical origin. These can be prevented with natural detoxification. I profess using aged garlic extract daily in my animals, sick or not, along with clean air and clean food.

What I have written for animals pertains to our own human health, as well. I and my family dogs and cats all take Kyolic daily.

Sincerely,

Gloria Dodd, DVM,
Gualala, CA

Editor's Note:
Here is how to reach Dr. Dodd's website: www.holisticvetpetcare.com
Her E-mail address is Everglow@MCN.org

Chapter 9

Aged Garlic – The Inside Story

Everybody knows that one and one make two. However, not everybody knows that one and one can add up to much more than that, if each one is the right one. And two of the right ones got together in Japan shortly after World War II – idealists Eugen Schnell, a former professor of medicinal chemistry and pharmacy at Berlin University, and banker Manji Wakunaga.

Appointed the head of the Japanese Drug Administration, Dr. Schnell shuddered at what he saw – antibiotics so misused for prevention that they were unable to work in medical emergencies, medicines with high prices and low curative powers, and drugs with horrendous side effects that sickened or, even worse, killed some patients.

In German, the word "schnell" means "hurry", and that's exactly what Dr. Schnell did to cure a deathly ill Japanese drug industry. One of his first acts was to enlist help from humanitarian Manji Wakunaga, explaining the dire situation and the need for researching, developing and implementing garlic products for prevention and cure. After all, garlic had been an effective and reliable folk medicine for a wide range of ailments in numerous cultures for thousands of years and appeared to be safe. For too long in recent times, garlic had been limited to the kitchen cabinet. Now it also had to enter the medicine chest.

To reach and benefit multi-millions of people everywhere – to overcome resistance to it — the garlic supplement had to be a "sociable" product, one without a tell-tale odor. Creating it would be an inflexible goal for company biochemists.

Better Than the Best

Meetings with Dr. Schnell lit a fire in Mr. Wakunaga, who founded a new Japanese industry, Wakunaga Pharmaceutical. For full appreciation of bonus values Wakunaga has developed in its products, it is necessary to know more about garlic. A hardy perennial, garlic – one of the world's oldest cultivated plants – is native to central Asia and the Mediterranean regions of Europe and Africa. A member of the lily family, along with its relatives – onions, leeks, chives and shallots – garlic, in botanical language, is called allium sativa. Cloves of garlic in a bulb are tightly fitted inside a paper-thin membrane and are garlic seeds.

Garlic as usual was not good enough for Mr. Wakunaga. He insisted on top quality from the ground up. Starting with the best seeds that money could buy, he chose special ground on the northern island of Hokkaido, rich organic soil – soil that had never known synthetic fertilizers, insecticides, fungicides and herbicides.

Over and above this, he insisted on using natural fertilizers – animal manure, rice bran, bark, and grass — and on rotation of crops so that Wakunaga's garlic could develop the richest content of nutrients. First, garlic is planted. In the next year it's wheat, and in the third, it's corn, then back to garlic.

Cloves planted in the rich volcanic soil each September are hardy descendants of the prime cloves from the first crop. Snow begins to whiten the plantings in October and blankets them for almost six months. The healthiest survive and flourish. These are the bulbs harvested at full maturity and used for Kyolic aged garlic extract.

Constantly monitored growth of the plants also assures users of the highest possible quality garlic, impossible for other companies that don't grow their own product Once harvested, the garlic is sliced then minced and placed in large, round, glistening, stainless steel tanks where it is aged for no less than 20 months. A near magical change takes place. Unique sulfur compounds develop that are conspicuously absent in traditionally processed garlic. These are S-allylmercapto cysteine, fructosyl arginine -- potent anti-oxidants – carboline, a free radical scavenger, protein F-4 — immune stimulants and cancer-fighters.

The final water and oil-soluble product is called Kyolic. The cold aging process was adapted and refined from a system used for centuries in China and Iran and other middle-eastern countries.

Aging, Quality Control, and Testing

Two towering results come from cold aging. The garlic increases its number of sulfur ingredients and their potency, enhancing their preventive and healing power, and, triumph of triumphs, loses its garlic odor! Now people throughout the world can breathe easy, secure that health-promoting garlic supplements won't undermine their social lives or careers.

(If you would like to age your garlic, please turn to the next section of the book and Lynn Allison's play-by-play description of one effective way of doing this.).

From start to finish, Wakunaga garlic is subjected to 250 quality control tests to assure its highest purity, uniformity and potency. More than three decades of extensive clinical studies – three hundred university and private lab research projects – many double-blind – prove the efficacy of aged garlic extract and supply new inputs to Wakunaga's prominent scientists, physicians and biochemists, who continue to study for product improvement and new product development in the company's $20 million research center in Japan and in another in Southern California.

Now Wakunaga garlic is also grown in the United States under identical conditions to those in Japan – from planting, harvesting and aging to the strict quality control testing. Independent assays show that it has the same nutrient content as that grown in Japan.

Experts Disqualify Allicin

When shopping for a garlic product, some consumers are confused about claims and counter-claims about the ingredient allicin. One faction insists that allicin is important in garlic's ability to prevent or cope with various ailments. Another, spearheaded by most garlic authorities, insists that it is nothing of the kind, that allicin escapes soon after raw garlic is crushed.

Kyolic garlic contains no allicin, and inasmuch as aged garlic has been tested and shown to be a success in 300-plus solid studies — vastly more than garlic of all other companies put together – Wakunaga states that allicin is not a preventive or curative ingredient.

While chairing the First World Congress on Garlic, Dr. Robert I. San-Lin voiced the ethical point that certain firms are marketing their products on dubious claims.

"Allicin is a transient and highly unstable compound, and no garlic product contains detectable amounts of allicin. There is no evidence showing that allicin is the active compound in garlic."

More Negative Reactions

Dr. San-Lin emphasized that many studies, including those presented to the Congress, demonstrate that compounds other than allicin are the key pharmacological and nutritional factors. "Allicin has little direct contribution to garlic's pharmacological and nutritional properties," he stated. "The claim that allicin is the only active principle of garlic is unfounded."

In a paper presented at a conference called, "Recent Advances on the Nutritional Benefits Accompanying the Use of Garlic as a Supplement, Dr. Harunobu Amagase reported:

"Allicin is an odorous and extremely unstable compound that decomposes to sulfides, including ajoene and dithins." In test tube studies, allicin has been shown to be an effective agent against microorganisms, but its effects in animals and human beings is questionable," he continued.

"Within a few minutes after you add allicin to blood, it can no longer be detected. Allicin cannot be detected in the urine after the ingestion of garlic or pure allicin. Although freshly crushed garlic contains a limited amount of allicin, no commercially available processed garlic preparations contain allicin." [1]

Disappearing Act of Allicin

Various other authorities agree that allicin is not an important factor in garlic's health protectiveness in that there are no detectable amounts of it in the blood after one eats raw garlic.

Dr. Earl Mindell writes, "Researchers have concluded, then, that allicin is not bioavailable – cannot be used by the body – and does not seem to be a biologically active compound of garlic." [2]

"Beware of products that promote their allicin content," writes Robert C. Atkins, MD, in *Dr. Atkins' Vita-Nutrient Solution.* "Allicin is a short-lived substance formed by crushing fresh garlic. It is not absorbed by the digestive tract – and for good reason: it damages red blood cells, and irritates body tissues, lab studies report." He recommends that readers "try an extract of aged garlic, either in capsule or as a liquid. Odorless and tasteless, it's the form that researchers have studied most extensively."

Morton Walker, DPM, tells us that "while *in vitro* studies may show allicin to be fungicidal, taken *in vivo* (in live human beings) it has no positive pharmacological effects." [3]

Dr. Willis R. Brewer, professor emeritus and dean of the University of Arizona College of Pharmacy, states: "Allicin is unstable and decomposes rapidly at room temperature." [4]

An investigation by the *Toronto Star*, one of Canada's most respected newspapers, revealed that three garlic supplements boasting allicin on their labels contained none. [5]

A prestigious scientific publication (*Journal of Agricultural Food Chemistry*:43: 2332-2338 (1995) has presented advanced research that conclusively proves no garlic supplement contains allicin – not a trace. And that's good news, because allicin, applied topically, can cause oxidative damage to the cells and tissues, and whose body needs that?

Unsolicited Aged Garlic Testimonials

In addition, recent research conducted by major universities and research institutes demonstrates the benefits of a complex assortment of safe, antioxidant, water-soluble compounds. (*Planta Medica* 60: 417-420 (1994). This research verifies the synergistic value of these sulfhydrals, including the marker compound S-allyl-cysteine and fructosyl-Arginine – the latter a powerful antioxidant only proved to be in aged garlic extract.

Dr. Vivienne Reeve, a Senior Research Fellow at Sydney University (Australia), who attended the first World Congress on Garlic in the USA, admits to being astonished when the keynote speaker, Dr. William Blot, of the National Cancer Institute, mentioned the broad range of diseases for which the right garlic has been found effective.

"The right garlic is aged garlic," he announced. [6]

On another pertinent subject, some companies claim to sell odorless garlic without putting their garlic through the costly, time-consuming, cold-aging process. They mask the odor by chemical and enteric coatings. However, when the capsules or tablets dissolve, they may leave garlic breath and a body odor that escapes through the pores. So, buyer beware! You could be paying a high tab for bad breath and offensive body odor.

Several Forms of Garlic

These commentaries stress that, like all men, all garlic is not created equal. It is critically important to know the inequalities to derive full values – especially, inasmuch as research by Hartman and New Hope shows that of 91 herbal supplements on the market, garlic was found to be used more than twice as much as its nearest competitor: ginseng.

Let's take a quick look at the various forms of garlic products – essential oil, dehydrated powder, oil macerate and extract, based on a paper published by the American Society for Nutritional Sciences. [7]

Essential Oil

Garlic essential oil is prepared in the following way. Whole garlic cloves are ground in water, steam-distilled or extracted in a solvent such as hexane. It is essentially reduced to a fraction of its original values to obtain the oil. Research-proved, beneficial, water-soluble compounds are eliminated. Some garlic oil products are diluted with other vegetable oil, so the amount of garlic present is diminished.

Dehydrated Powder

Garlic cloves are sliced, crushed, diced, dried and pulverized into powder as the flavoring for condiments and processed foods. Processing is like a toll gate that exacts a price. That price in this instance is a loss of many of the beneficial water-soluble sulfur compounds that stimulate and invigorate the immune system. Dehydrated garlic retains some of the constituents of raw garlic, but these vary according to each product. Greater standardization is necessary.

Oil Macerate

Intended originally for use in condiments, garlic oil macerate is marketed as a supplement. Whole garlic cloves are ground into vegetable oils. Some of the effective substances are retained. However, again, standardization for ingredients has not been pursued adequately.

Extract

Aged garlic is the only garlic on the market processed differently from the other three types of garlic extract, as described earlier in this chapter. After separation of the solution, the extract is concentrated.

No Toxic Effects

Aged garlic contains mainly water-soluble sulfur compounds such as SAC and SAMC, along with a variety of oil-soluble sulfur compounds. SAC can be used for standardization because, it is bioavailable.

For greatest preventive and health benefits, supplements must often be used for long periods, so the question of toxicity arises. The safety of AGE has been confirmed by various toxicological studies. A toxicity test of aged garlic by the U.S. Food and Drug Administration revealed no adverse effects, nor did seven clinical studies conducted on 1000 volunteers.

Here are guidelines for the correct intake of aged garlic. All adults need to do is follow the suggested amounts mentioned on the labels. The recommended amounts are one capsule of liquid Kyolic (a quarter of a teaspoon) three times daily. It is different for children of all age groups. The following are the daily amounts suggested by Wakunaga of America according to age groups:

1-6 months: Start with 1-2 drops in a liquid (formula, juice or water), once a day, for 1-2 weeks. If well tolerated, this dosage may be increased gradually to an eighth to a quarter of a teaspoon.

6-18 months: Start at 2-3 drops in a liquid for 1-2 weeks. If well tolerated. The dosage may be increased gradually to about one-quarter to one-half teaspoon.

18 months – 3 years: Start out at 3-4 drops in liquid for 1-2 weeks. If well tolerated, the dosage may be increased gradually to about one-quarter to one-half teaspoon.

3+ years: Start out at one-quarter of a teaspoon for 1-2 weeks. If well tolerated, the dosage may be increased gradually to half teaspoon.

After an infant/child has been taking Kyolic for a time, the liquid may be put into their food instead of their liquids. Also, the daily amount of aged garlic may be given all at one time or in two or more servings.

The liquid formula is more readily absorbed and contains constituents which could not be retained in the dehydration process to generate the powdered form. In addition, the liquid formula was used in the majority of the studies done on Kyolic.

The suggested intake for Kyolic odorless aged garlic extract is indicated on the assorted formulas and ranges from 1-4 capsules/tablets per day for adults (600-1400 mg/day). Children's dosages can be adjusted according to individual tolerance (generally, up to half of the adult dosage.)

Garlic has been widely and safely used in cooking for centuries and çontinues to be – with the only penalty to the eater, a breath that won't dissipate its telltale evidence for at least 24-hours, despite parsley, mints, or tingly mouthwashes. However, most of us accept this as one of those trade-offs in life.

Some decades ago, the countless health contributions of garlic were only folk medicine when an 11-year American Medical Association study of the heavily Italian population of Roseto, Pennsylvania was carried out. This research produced an astonishing result. Despite the Roseto citizens' high intake of saturated fats – foods cooked and fried in butter and lard — and their frequent eating of prosciutto ham with its inch wide border of white fat, they showed better than average heart and artery conditions. [8]

Were blood levels of cholesterol and fats skyhigh? Guess again. Cholesterol levels averaged 224, about the same as those of people covered in the Framingham study. Heart attacks in under-55 year old Roseto men were almost non-existent. And, among the small number of over-65 years of age men who endured heart attacks, there was a high rate of recovery and survival.

Today conditions in Roseto are changing. Family ties are not as close as during the period of the study reported above. Therefore, selection and preparation of foods is not as uniform, so health and wellness results differ somewhat.

Recipes Galore

Ever-present garlic in many Italian dishes and its vast contribution to the health of the Roseto population were not given sufficient importance years ago, because most of the studies demonstrating the inestimable values of garlic took place a generation later.

Let's face it. A healthful diet is the solid base for a supplement such as aged garlic. That's why this book wouldn't be complete if it didn't offer recipes featuring garlic ala Roseto, Rome and Athens. Although Lynn Allison contributed a generous share of the research and writing to this section of the book, the following section will be hers exclusively, because it features autobiographical information and 139 of her heavenly gourmet garlic recipes which are the talk of Florida, where she lives.

A tribute to her is the great taste of her recipes and frequent return dinner visits of relatives and friends. However, they don't leave her guests breathless, as does aged garlic. Further, even wide-open windows and brisk breezes can't dissipate the evidence that garlic is eaten there.

Well, now we turn you over to Lynn Allison and her ever-so-garlicky recipes.

Chapter 10

Heavenly Garlic Gourmet Recipes

A song of praise for garlic . . .
Opens new doors to its glories . . .
Anyone who takes health and food
seriously must have it!

Fran White, Herbalist

Garlic has always been a key part of my life – probably due to my Greek heritage. (Mediterranean people love garlic in their cuisine.) The flavor and aroma of garlic have delighted me ever since I graduated to solid foods. However, now that I've researched and written about the amazing healing powers of garlic, I'm even more of a garlic fanatic.

I grew up with the odor of freshly-peeled garlic cloves scenting the air, as my grandmother prepared Skordalia, a traditional Greek dish made with lots of the pungent herbs. I can still see my father mincing garlic cloves for my mother's famous Greek Lentil Soup, a delicacy I continue to prepare. (Please see how to make Skordalia and Greek Lentil Soup among my recipes that follow).

There's nothing quite as tantalizing as a garlic-laced stew simmering on the stove or the succulent aroma of a garlic-enhanced roast in the oven. To the garlic lover, garlic belongs in almost every dish. Somebody did the virtually impossible at one of the annual Garlic Fairs at Gilroy, California. He created garlic ice cream!

Thanks to my garlic-scented memory, I vividly recall a time

when my love of garlic proved socially embarrassing. I was dating a rather staid fellow whose very proper family frowned upon odoriferous garlic.

I had to choose between him and garlic and . . . well, you can't take the herb out of the gal. Bye, bye, boy friend! Over the years, the gap between garlic lovers and non garlic lovers has narrowed, thanks to the increasing use and enjoyment of the taste of garlic in homes and restaurants and growing evidence of its health-giving powers.

Garlic and Love

Fortunately, I married an Italian man whose love for garlic even exceeds my own! He carefully inserts slivers of garlic into our roasts, and adds crushed garlic to our dogs' food, because we know that garlic repels fleas — vampires, too, just in case Count Dracula is still around. He liberally rubs the salad bowl with a cut clove of garlic to give our Caesar salads extra zip.

Every gourmet cook I know reveres garlic. An accomplished chef and friend of mine, Tony Damiano, formerly of New York City's famous Russian Tea Room, uses garlic extensively to flavor his illustrious specialties. Tony, who now operates his own restaurant, Damiano's at Tarrimore House in Delray Beach, Florida, says:

"I lost 60 pounds simply by using less fat and more flavoring in my cuisine. Garlic plays an important role in creating both subtle and assertive flavors in almost any dish I create. Using garlic with other herbs, notably ginger and coriander, in Asian cuisine, creates a symphony of flavor."

Noel Kamburian, a famous Mediterranean chef, claims that garlic is absolutely instrumental in any dish he creates.

"You can't have a song without music," he rhapsodizes. "Similarly, you can't create great cuisine without garlic. It's in my veins. I believe my mother used garlic in my baby food." (Noel chose his mother wisely.)

In Celebration of Garlic

Our generation, in search for holistic ways to stay healthy, is revitalizing garlic as a popular healing food, restoring it to its rightful throne as king of designer foods that fight disease. Every year, the charts on garlic production and growth show a dramatic upward surge. This is proved by sales figures and the dozens of garlic festivals across the country each year. The Gilroy (California) Garlic Festival, held during the last weekend in July, tops them all. Located eighty miles south of San Francisco on Highway 101, Gilroy calls itself "The Garlic Capital of the World," because more garlic is grown and processed there than in any other region of the earth. When you're driving anywhere in the general vicinity of Gilroy, you don't have to see it to know its there. Common scents tell you.

A humorist of another age, Will Rogers, once claimed that Gilroy is "the only town in America where you can marinate a steak by hanging it on the clothesline."

There's more to the Gilroy Garlic Festival than garlic displays and serving of foods using it. You can compete in various activities – Garlic Golf, Love That Garlic Tennis Tournament, Miss Garlic Contest, and the Tour de Garlic Country Bicycle Tour. (For more information on the Gilroy Garlic Festival, write to PO Box 2311, Gilroy, California 95020.)

Not too many breaths away, in Berkeley, California, the Lovers of the Stinking Rose Society feature the Berkeley Garlic Festival, a two-week celebration annually in mid-July. More than 50 restaurants create unique garlic menus during this period. More information? Contact the Lovers of the Stinking Rose, 1621 Fifth Street, Berkeley, CA 94710.

The Stinking Rose and Garlic Festivals

Of course, the Stinking Rose restaurant in San Francisco is famous for its fabulous garlic-flavored menu. It needs no publicity. Natives and out-of-towners pack the place. And it's well worth packing. Even strangers have little trouble finding the place. If they get lost, all they have to do is follow their nose.

However, California has no monopoly on things garlic. The annual Garlic Fest in Covington, Kentucky, held in February, draws tens of thousands of garlic lovers, even though this is not a warm season. Highlight events there are a garlic bulb peeling contest, garlic cook-offs and a Miss Garlic beauty pageant. (For more information, write to Coving Haus, 100 West Sixth Street, Covington, Kentucky 41011.)

In Massachusetts, there's the annual Fitchburg Garlic Festival that's held every June in a most appropriate place – an Italian church!

Anybody who wants the maximum flavor from garlic cookery should know a little more about buying, storing, and preparing it – things I learned in a lifetime of observing my mother and grandmother's methods.

When you buy garlic, look for firm and plump bulbs with clean, dry, unbroken skin. Once you bring garlic home, store it in a cool, dry place in an open container — not in the refrigerator, because of the dampness.

You can also chop or puree garlic cloves and store them in jars. To preserve the flavor, mix a little olive oil; or lemon juice with them. Let the puree ripen for at least a day before using it for your favorite recipes. Garlic is a low calorie seasoning agent – just a few calories per clove.

Do you want to dehydrate it? Cut thin slices of the cloves and place them to dry in a gas oven with just the pilot light on. Once the slices become brittle, store them in a tightly sealed jar in a cool cupboard – never in the refrigerator. Marinating fresh garlic is easy. Cover sliced cloves with the best olive oil and include freshly sliced herbs and spices to your desired taste.

How to Peel and Cook Garlic

Some people make peeling garlic cloves difficult. There are easy ways to do this. Hit a clove with the flat side of a large knife blade, and then cut across the root end, peeling the skin upward. Twenty seconds in the microwave will also loosen the skin. If you need many cloves, just drop them in boiling water for two minutes, then plunge them into cold water and watch the peel just slip off. A best-selling product on the market is the garlic peeler.

To develop garlic's full-bodied flavor, cook it long and slowly. When sautéing garlic in a pan for a particular recipe, be careful not to scorch or burn it. This gives garlic an uncharacteristic bitter flavor. Gently sauté the cloves on medium to medium low heat for about three minutes – or until they become translucent.

You can also bake garlic cloves after removing their skin, drizzling them with olive oil, and sprinkling them with oregano, wrapping them with foil and baking them at 375 degrees for an hour. The nutty sweet cloves make an excellent and unusual appetizer that are great with roasted meat, fowl or fish.

A secret I learned from Italian chefs is a sumptuous garlic bread called "Bruschetta." You can make it by rubbing garlic cloves on the crusty perimeter of sliced and toasted bread and topping the slices with chopped tomatoes, mushrooms and olive oil.

Before we get to the recipes, let's deal with something that happens after you eat garlicky foods – breath with too much character. There's an old saying that "garlic breath is better than no breath at all." True, but let's consider ways to de-garlic garlic breath. Eat fresh parsley. Rinse your mouth with lemon juice. (This method works to a degree but has limitations. If you use it frequently, the acids in lemon juice can etch your teeth.)

Earlier, I promised to share a formula for aging your own garlic. It is not mine. Allen Beygi, of Escondido, California, graciously contributed it as a way that he seasons garlic for greater potency and less (if any) odor. This is offered with Allen's permission.

5 pounds fresh garlic
1/2 gallon distilled white vinegar
Waxed paper
4-5 tablespoons of salt
1 gallon size glass jar

1. Sterilize a 1 gallon-size glass jar.
2. Cut off bottom club (root area) of each garlic bunch.
3. Remove garlic husks (skin). Leave on the last skin areas. Vinegar will soften it.
4. Add 4-5 tablespoons salt to vinegar.
5. Bring 1/2 gallon salted vinegar to a boil.
6. Empty garlic into glass jar.
7. Very slowly add vinegar to garlic in glass jar so the jar will not crack.
8. Wait 1/2 hour and put waxed paper on top of jar, and then put on the plastic lid tightly.
9. Write a date on top of the jar.
10. One week later, add more vinegar. (If you have left-over cold vinegar, use this.
11. Store on a shelf for a minimum of 6 months. One to two years is much better. Perfect after three years. (It is not necessary to store this in a refrigerator.)

It's easy to include garlic in your food. Chop a few cloves and mix them with sun-dried tomatoes slathered on French bread for an instant bruschetta. Add garlic to your frying pan when putting together a quick stir-fry. Insert garlic cloves in roasts to give them a richer flavor. Always add garlic to your salad dressing!

With today's busy lifestyles, I've kept the recipes in this section short and simple. Feel free to use your own imagination and create new garlic-laced dishes for your family.

I think there is something truly beautiful about a family cooking dinner together and sitting around the table enjoying good food and conversation. I sincerely hope that you and your family will use these healthy recipes and benefit from the healing power of garlic!

Lynn Allison

Well, enough about aging garlic. Let's get on with my recipes that come in the following categories:

INDEX TO RECIPES

POULTRY

MEAT AND EGG DISHES

SEAFOOD

CROCKPOT RECIPES

MISCELLANEOUS

RECIPES

APPETIZERS

MUSHROOM BUTTONS

4 servings

Simple fare with a remarkable flavor – thanks to garlic!

1 lb. lg. mushrooms
1/4 cup chopped onion
2 cloves garlic, minced
1 Tbsp. grated Parmesan cheese

Pan Size: Casserole or pie pan *Oven Temp.: Broil* *Time: 5 minutes*

Preheat broiler. Wash mushrooms well and pat dry. Remove the stems and chop them finely. Sauté stems with onion and garlic in a non-stick frying pan over medium heat for 5 minutes. Fill caps with this mixture. Sprinkle with Parmesan cheese. Place mushrooms in a broiler-proof casserole or pie plate. Broil for 5 minutes. Serve warm.

NOTE: You may also add 1/2 cup chopped, fresh spinach to the stuffing mixture.

MICROWAVE VEGETABLE PLATTER

6 servings

So easy to prepare, but it looks like a dish for a king!

1 cup broccoli flowerets
1 cup cauliflower
1 cup carrot sticks
2 zucchini squash, cut into julienne sticks
1 red pepper, cut into strips
1 green pepper, cut into strips
1 Tbsp. lemon juice
2 Tbsp. minced garlic
Salt and freshly ground pepper, to taste

Pan Size: Plate *Microwave Temp.: High* *Time: 5 minutes*

Arrange the broccoli, cauliflower and carrot sticks around the outer edge of a microwave-proof plate or dish. Place the rest of the vegetables neatly in the center, in separate piles. Sprinkle with garlic and lemon juice. Cover with plastic wrap and microwave on high for 5 minutes. Let stand 5 minutes before serving.

ANTIPASTO SALAD

2 servings

This appetizer or light luncheon is great for the single student or solitary diner who wants taste and nutrition with little fuss and effort.

2 cups chopped fresh broccoli
2 cups chopped cauliflower
1 - 6 oz. can water-packed tuna, drained
1 tsp. minced garlic
4 carrots, cut into 1/4 inch slices
1/4 cup fat-free Italian salad dressing
2 cups romaine lettuce

Steam the broccoli and cauliflower, about 3 minutes, until tender-crisp. Mix the tuna, garlic and vegetables with the dressing until well blended. Chill at least 30 minutes. Serve atop the romaine. This mixture is also good spooned into a pita bread for lunch.

BAKED STUFFED TOMATO

4 servings

You can double, triple or otherwise multiply this recipe.

4 med. tomatoes
1 cup chopped broccoli, steamed or microwaved until crisp
1 tsp. minced garlic
2 Tbsp. soft bread crumbs
1 tsp. oregano
2 Tbsp. grated Parmesan cheese
Salt and freshly-ground pepper, to taste

Pan Size: Baking dish *Oven Temp.: 400°* *Time: 5 minutes*

Preheat oven. Cut tomatoes in half and scoop out pulp. Combine pulp, broccoli, garlic, salt, pepper, bread crumbs and oregano. Stuff each tomato half with broccoli mixture and sprinkle with Parmesan cheese. Bake until bubbly.

EGGPLANT PROVENCALE

8 servings

Here's a side dish or appetizer that's sure to please.

5 med. eggplants, peeled and chopped
Salt and pepper, to taste
1 cup olive oil
6 ripe tomatoes, chopped and seeds removed
7 cloves garlic, finely chopped
1 Tbsp. thyme
1/4 cup seasoned Italian bread crumbs
4 anchovy fillets
1 Tbsp. flour
1/4 cup milk

Pan Size: 2-qt. casserole *Oven Temp.: 350°* *Time: 30 minutes*

Sprinkle the eggplant with a little salt and pepper. In a large skillet, heat 1/2 cup olive oil and sauté the eggplant, tomatoes, garlic and thyme. Stir in the bread crumbs. Continue cooking over medium-low heat while mashing the vegetables with a fork until they are tender.

In a small skillet, heat the remaining oil with the anchovies. Add the flour and mix well. Stir in the milk. Stir the anchovy mixture into the eggplant mixture and transfer the whole mixture into a buttered casserole dish. Bake until golden. Serve hot.

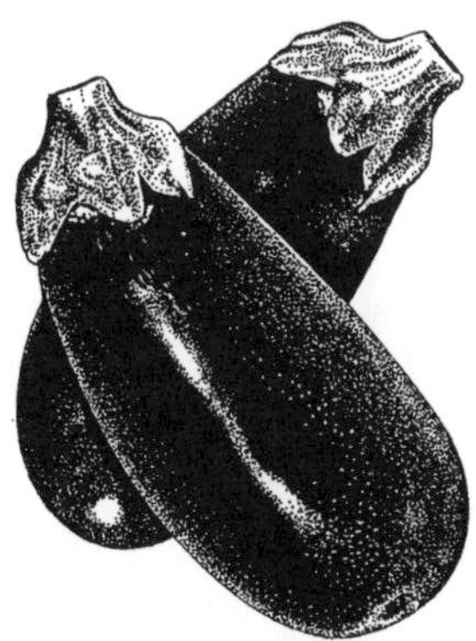

CURRY DIP

Makes 1-1/2 cups

Here's another exotic dip that has great flavor, thanks to the subtle addition of garlic.

1 cup low-fat cottage cheese
1 sm. tomato, chopped
1/2 cup fresh parsley
1 tsp. curry powder (or more, if you like spicy food)
1 scallion, chopped
3 cloves garlic, minced

Combine all ingredients in a blender and process until smooth. Chill well before serving.

SWEET POTATO CHIPS

These yummy snacks are healthy, yet flavorful. You'll never want a commercially prepared potato chip again!

2 lbs. yams or sweet potatoes, scrubbed and sliced 1/8 inch thick
2 Tbsp. safflower oil
2 Tbsp. spicy vegetable seasoning like Spike or Mrs. Dash
1 Tbsp. garlic salt

Pan Size: Baking sheet *Oven Temp.: 450°* *Time: 12 to 15 minutes*

Place sliced potatoes in a bowl, sprinkle with oil and mix thoroughly. Spread the potatoes in a single layer on a non-stick baking sheet and sprinkle with vegetable seasoning and garlic salt. Bake until nicely browned. Serve immediately.

NOTE: Baking potatoes can also be used to make oven fries that are simply delicious. I sometimes dip the raw slices in low-calorie Italian dressing instead of oil before baking and sprinkle a little paprika on top for extra zip.

ROASTED GARLIC BEAN DIP

Makes 2 cups

An excellent appetizer dip that's great with pita bread.

5 cloves roasted garlic*
1 - 15 oz. can cannellini, drained
1 Tbsp. cider vinegar
1/2 tsp. ground cumin
1/2 to 3/4 cup low-fat yogurt
2 Tbsp. chopped parsley

In a food processor, combine garlic, beans, vinegar and cumin. Process 1 minute, scraping bowl once. Add yogurt and parsley; process until just blended, adding more yogurt if needed.

Serve with crackers or warm pita bread cut into sections and warmed in the oven.

*NOTE: To make roasted garlic, coat unpeeled cloves with olive oil. Bake at 375° for 15 minutes. Cool and peel.

VARIATION: You can use plain, peeled garlic.

CHICK PEA SPREAD

Makes 2 cups

This low-fat dip is great with crackers or veggies. Vary the spices to suit your taste.

1/2 cup non-fat plain yogurt
1 - 14 oz. can chick peas, drained
2 Tbsp. lemon juice
1 Tbsp. minced garlic
1/2 tsp. curry powder, optional

In a blender, purée all the ingredients, starting with the yogurt and some of the chick peas and adding more until well blended. Spoon into a serving dish. Serve with sesame crackers or pita bread.

SPINACH DIP

Makes 2-1/2 cups

This versatile dip is great warm or cold. Serve with toasted pita bread.

1 cup non-fat yogurt
1 Tbsp. minced garlic
1 Tbsp. chopped fresh dill
1 - 10 oz. pkg. frozen chopped spinach, thawed and well drained*
1 cup shredded Cheddar cheese (can be low-fat)

Mix all ingredients together in a small bowl. If you want to serve it hot, microwave the dip for 1 minute on high. If you're going to serve it cold, chill at least 1 hour before serving.

*NOTE: To drain spinach, place in a sieve and squeeze dry with your hands until all water is removed.

BLUE CHEESE BITES

6 servings

You can double or triple the recipe to serve a crowd!

1 - 10 oz. pkg. buttermilk biscuits (from the dairy case)
1/2 cup crumbled blue cheese
1/4 cup melted margarine
1 tsp. minced garlic

Pan Size: Cookie sheet *Oven Temp.: 400°* *Time: 15 minutes*

Preheat oven. Separate biscuits and cut into quarters. Place on a non-stick cookie sheet, 1 inch apart. Sprinkle with blue cheese, melted margarine and garlic. Bake until golden brown.

SPICY YOGURT DIP

Makes 1 cup

This excellent dip tastes like it's made with sour cream but doesn't have the fat and calories of the real thing. It's great for chicken wings, raw vegetables – anything that needs a dip with a real bite!

2/3 cup plain low-fat yogurt
1/3 cup sour cream
1 tsp. paprika
1 Tbsp. minced garlic
1 tsp. lemon juice
1/4 tsp. white pepper

In a bowl, combine all the ingredients, stirring them well. Chill the dip, covered, for 1 hour or longer before serving.

VARIATION: Omit paprika and replace with 1/4 cup chopped fresh dill.

MOCK CRAB DIP

Makes 1-1/2 cups

M-M-good! And it doesn't hurt your pocketbook either!

8 oz. low-fat cottage cheese
1 Tbsp. minced onion or scallions
1 tsp. lemon juice
4 oz. imitation crab (surimi)
1 tsp. Worcestershire sauce
1 Tbsp. minced garlic

Shred crab meat with a fork. Combine all ingredients and chill, covered. Serve with whole wheat crackers and/or raw vegetable sticks.

SPICY ARTICHOKE HEART DIP

Makes 4 cups

A quick and easy appetizer that's best served with toasted garlic bread.

1 can artichoke hearts, rinsed and squeezed dry
2 cups salsa
1 clove garlic, minced
1 tsp. oregano or Italian herb blend
A few drops hot pepper sauce
1 Tbsp. fresh parsley, for garnish

Chop artichoke hearts fine. Combine all the ingredients, except parsley, in a bowl. Stir to blend. Sprinkle with parsley and chill at least one hour in the refrigerator before serving.

QUEBEC TOURTIERE

2-crust pie pastry
1-1/4 lbs. ground beef and pork
3/4 cups water
1 onion, chopped
1/2 cup chopped celery
2 Tbsp. chopped garlic
1 tsp. black pepper
2 Tbsp. liquid gravy maker
1/4 tsp. rosemary, to taste
1/4 tsp. ketchup, to taste
1/4 tsp. Worcestershire sauce
Cinnamon and nutmeg, to taste
1/4 cup old-fashioned rolled oats
1 egg yolk beaten with
1 Tbsp. milk

Pan Size: Pie pan *Oven Temp.: 425°* *Time: 15 minutes*
Oven Temp.: 375° *Time: 25 minutes*

In a large saucepan, mix meat with water and bring to a boil; add vegetables and seasonings and cook, partially covered, over medium low heat for 30 minutes, adding more water if necessary. Stir in oats; cool. Drain off fat. Spoon into pastry shell, cover with top crust; crimp edges, brush with egg-milk mixture. Cut steam vents bottom and bake in preheated oven until crust is golden.

TZATZIKI

Makes 2 cups

This wonderful dip is always the hit of my parties. Use it to make a delicious spread for pita sandwiches as well.

1 cucumber, peeled, seeded and chopped
2 cups non-fat plain yogurt
2 cloves garlic, peeled and chopped
4 Tbsp. fresh dill, chopped

Combine all ingredients and store in an airtight container. Serve well chilled with fresh veggies or pita bread.

ANTIPASTO

Makes 8 servings

My husband surprised me one day by buying the ingredients for this wonderful appetizer which we served to company one night. One fellow ate the entire stock of prosciutto ham! Next time, we'll buy more! All the ingredients can be purchased at your local deli or supermarket.

8 thin slices salami
8 thin slices prosciutto
2 carrots, sliced into 2 inch sticks
2 celery sticks, sliced into
  2 inch sticks
8 black Calamata olives
8 lg. green garlic olives
8 slices Mozzarella
16 sm. cherry tomatoes
2 cloves garlic, minced
1/2 cup Italian dressing

Roll the cold cuts and cheese tightly, like a jelly roll and fasten with toothpicks. Arrange neatly on a round platter. Combine the garlic and dressing; shake well. Drizzle the antipasto with the garlic-laced dressing. Serve with cocktail napkins or set out small plates.

QUICHE

6 servings

This basic quiche recipe can be altered to suit your purposes. Feel free to experiment with different fillings.

1 unbaked 9-inch pie shell
1 Tbsp. butter
2 lg. scallions, sliced
2 cloves garlic, chopped
4 slices bacon, chopped
3 eggs
1-1/2 cups milk
1/2 tsp. paprika
1 cup shredded low-fat cheese
Salt and freshly-ground pepper,
  to taste

Pan Size: Pie pan *Oven Temp.: 400°* *Time: 40 minutes*

Preheat oven. In a large frying pan, heat butter over medium heat until melted. Stir in scallions, garlic and bacon. Stir and cook over medium heat for 5 minutes or until bacon is crisp.

Meanwhile, in a blender, mix eggs, milk and salt until smooth. Place the bacon mixture in the pie shell. Pour the yogurt mixture over the bacon. Sprinkle the cheese and spices over the top and bake until set.

VARIATION #1: Add chopped spinach, seafood or just about any leftover vegetable (sliced zucchini is superb!) to the pie shell before adding the yogurt-milk mixture. I love adding 1 pkg. of defrosted and drained frozen spinach and 1 cup of surimi or crab meat.

VARIATION #2: Eliminate the scallions and add 2 cups chopped onion for a very tasty quiche.

CHICKEN LIVER PATE

Makes 3 cups

Garlic in Mama's chicken liver! Why not?
It adds a very special flavor to this traditional recipe.

1 lb. chicken livers
2 cups water
1 onion, quartered
2 hard-boiled eggs
1/2 cup fresh parsley, minced
2 cloves garlic, minced
2 Tbsp. brandy
Salt and freshly-ground pepper, to taste

Boil chicken livers 10 minutes in water. Add more water if necessary to keep from sticking. Cover and let stand 10 minutes. Process the livers with the remaining ingredients in a blender or food processor, adding a little water from the cooking liquid to make a fine paste.

NOTE: For extra flavor, you can also sauté the livers in butter or chicken fat instead of boiling. Add the livers and the butter drippings to the blender or food processor.

SPICY MEATBALLS

6 servings

Appetizers that are quick to prepare, yet taste great.

1 lb. lean ground round or turkey
1 - 1 oz. pkt. onion soup mix
1/2 cup ketchup or chili sauce
1/2 cup flour or bread crumbs
1 tsp. minced garlic
1 tsp. dried oregano
Salt and freshly-ground pepper, to taste

Pan Size: Microwave dish *Temp.: HIGH* *Time: 10 minutes*

Mix all ingredients together and form into 1-inch balls. Place in a microwave dish. Cover with vented plastic and wrap; microwave on HIGH for 10 minutes, turning the dish twice during cooking. Drain off excess fat and liquid. Serve meatballs with toothpicks.

NOTE: You can also sauté these in a 12-inch skillet. Brown the meatballs over high heat, then simmer for 15 minutes, adding a cup of water or bouillon to the pan.

BAKED GARLIC

8 servings

8 whole heads fresh garlic
2 to 4 Tbsp. olive oil
4 sprigs fresh rosemary or oregano, or 2 tsp. dried

Pan Size: Baking dish *Oven Temp.: 350°* *Time: 1 hour*

Preheat oven. Remove outer layers of skin from garlic, leaving cloves and head intact. Place all heads on double thickness of foil; top with olive oil and herbs. Fold up and seal. Bake. Serve one whole head per person. Squeeze cooked cloves from skin onto cooked meats or vegetables or on toasted French bread.

VARIATIONS: You may trim tops off heads to expose tops of garlic cloves. This makes cloves easier to scoop out. then, bake as directed. Cooking time will be slightly reduced.

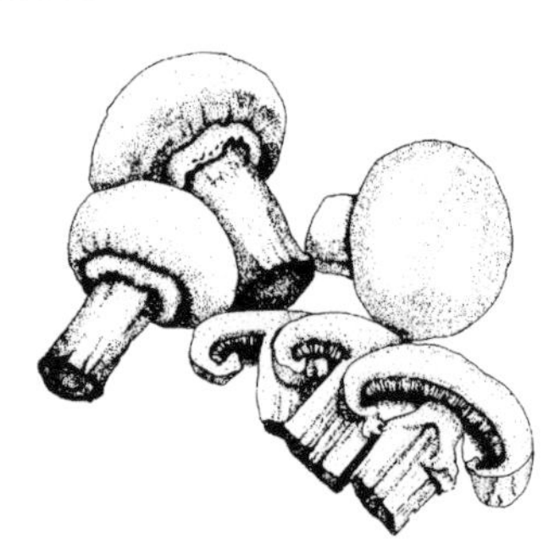

MUSHROOM AND GARLIC IN PUFF PASTRY

4 servings

This elegant dish is extremely easy to prepare and a delight to serve.

2 Tbsp. olive oil
4 garlic cloved, minced
1 med. onion, diced
1 med. tomato, chopped
1 lb. mushrooms, cleaned and sliced
2 lg. eggs, beaten
1/4 cup heavy cream
1/2 lb. store-bought puff pastry

Pan Size: Lasagna or jelly roll pan
Oven Temp.: 400° *Time: 10 + 25 minutes*

Preheat oven. Heat oil in a large skillet over medium heat and add the garlic, onion and tomato. Simmer for 10 minutes. Add the mushrooms and cook, uncovered, 7 minutes more. Remove from heat and cool. Stir in the egg and cream.

Spread or roll the thawed puff pastry into an 11X4 inch rectangle, line a shallow pan and bake for 10 minutes, or until lightly puffed. Prick the pastry gently with a fork to deflate it. Spread the mushroom mixture over the shell and bake for 25 minutes. Let cool for 5 minutes before slicing.

SOUPS

Garlic lends a special appeal to soups, giving them an unequaled richness of flavor. Here's a sampling of both hot and cold soups that owe their tastiness to garlic.

SPANISH GARLIC SOUP

4 servings

This light first-course soup wins top honors for flavor and health-giving properties. You can also use it as a stock to make other dishes such as rice, beans or pasta.

12 cloves garlic, peeled and chopped
1 tsp. salt
1 tsp. white pepper
1/4 tsp. oregano
1/4 tsp. thyme
1/4 tsp. basil
1 bay leaf
5 cups chicken stock
2 Tbsp. olive oil
2 slices whole grain bread, toasted
Grated Parmesan cheese, to taste (Optional)

Combine garlic, seasonings, stock, and oil and bring to a boil in a 5-quart saucepan. Cover and simmer for 30 minutes. Crumble bread into the soup and return to a boil. Serve as is, or topped with grated cheese.

FRENCH GARLIC SOUP

16 servings

The French region of Provence boasts liberal use of garlic in its cuisine. This great soup has lots of aromatic garlic!

2 Tbsp. olive oil
1 cup chopped garlic
1/4 cup chopped shallots
2 med. carrots, chopped fine
1/2 cup flour
1 cup dry red wine
1 gal. chicken stock
2 bay leaves
2 Tbsp. minced parsley
1-1/2 cups lentils
Salt and freshly-ground pepper, to taste

In a large stock pot, heat the olive oil over medium heat and sauté the garlic, shallots and carrots until tender. Add flour and mix well. Add the wine and stir until smooth. Add the stock, bay leaves, parsley and lentils. Bring the mixture to a boil and simmer, covered, until lentils are tender (about 25 minutes). Season with salt and pepper.

GREEK LENTIL SOUP

8 servings

Being of Greek descent, I am particularly fond of this soup.

2 Tbsp. olive oil
2 med. onions, chopped
2 stalks celery, chopped
2 carrots, chopped
8 cups water
1 - 6 oz. can tomato paste
2 cloves garlic, chopped
1 bay leaf
2 cups dried lentils
4 cups shredded spinach
Salt and white pepper, to taste
3 Tbsp. lemon juice

Heat oil in a large saucepan and sauté onion until soft. Add remaining ingredients except spinach and lemon juice. Mix well. Bring to a boil; cover and simmer 1 hour. Add spinach and seasonings to taste and cook 10 minutes more. Stir in lemon juice and serve.

VEGETABLE CLAM CHOWDER

Makes 4 servings for a main dish or
8 servings as an appetizer

My husband LOVES clam chowder, so I made it healthy. This is my easy, weeknight version of a chowder he can make in 30 minutes. It's low in fat and very tasty. Serve with garlic bread and a good Caesar salad. It's a meal in itself!

2 cups water
2 tsp. chicken bouillon granules, low sodium, if possible
1 - 10 oz. pkg. frozen spinach
2 carrots, peeled, scraped and sliced thinly
2 celery stalks, sliced thinly
5 garlic cloves, peeled
1/2 lb. mushrooms, sliced
1 - 16 oz. can low-fat New England Clam Chowder
1 - 10 oz. can clams, with juice
1 tsp. Worcestershire sauce
2 Tbsp. freshly squeezed lemon juice
Freshly ground black pepper, to taste

Pan Size: 2-qt. microwavable casserole Temp.: HIGH Time: 15 + 5 minutes
Temp.: 60% Time: 10 minutes

In casserole, add water, bouillon, carrots, celery spinach and garlic. Microwave, uncovered, for 15 minutes. Add mushrooms and microwave for 5 more minutes. Stir. Add the can of chowder, the can of clams and the Worcestershire sauce, lemon juice and black pepper. Microwave at 60% power for 10 minutes. Serve in heated dishes.

MISO VEGETABLE SOUP

Makes 8 servings

I couldn't believe it when my meat-and-potato husband asked for more of this heart-healthy soup that's rich in B-vitamins. You can find red miso in the refrigerated section of your health food store. Serve this soup with a good sour dough bread and you've got a meal and a half! Please feel free to add your own touches: some leftover corn, fish, or any other ingredients you have on hand!

8 cups water
4 Tbsp. red miso
2 onions, chopped
4 carrots, peeled and sliced
4 celery stalks, sliced
4 cloves garlic, peeled and chopped
1 lb. kale, washed well and chopped*
1 lg. potato, peeled and chopped coarsely
1 - 16 oz. can lentils, drained
Black pepper, to taste

In a large soup kettle, heat the water to boiling. Add the remaining ingredients, lower the heat to medium and simmer for 30 minutes with the top slightly ajar. Stir once or twice during cooking. Cool and reheat before serving to develop flavors.

*NOTE: A 16-oz. pkg. of frozen spinach or a bunch of collard greens can be substituted.

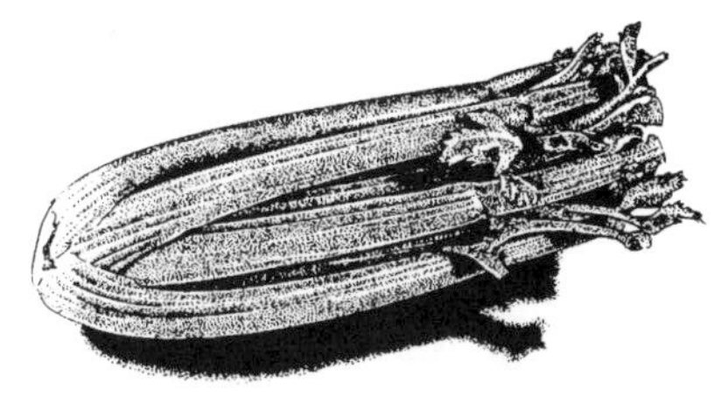

EASY VEGETABLE SOUP

4 servings

This quick, healthful soup tastes like it was simmered for hours.

2 med. carrots, cut into 1/2-inch slices
2 stalks celery, cut into 1-inch slices
1/2 cup chopped onion
3 cloves garlic, chopped
2 cups water, divided
2 cups tomato juice
1 tsp. soy sauce
1 tsp. oregano
1 Tbsp. butter or olive oil
Salt and pepper, to taste

Place carrots, celery and onion into a blender with 1 cup water. Process until smooth. Combine second cup of water and all remaining ingredients, except butter, in a saucepan and bring to a boil. Cover and simmer for 5 minutes. Remove from heat and stir in butter or oil. Season to taste.

STRACCIATELLA

6 servings

Add cooked chicken or shrimp for a one-dish meal.

2 cloves garlic
6 cups chicken broth
1 tsp. salt, or to taste
6 cups shredded greens, such as cabbage, spinach or escarole
2 eggs
1/4 cup grated Parmesan cheese
1/2 cup seasoned croutons, homemade or purchased

Peel and chop garlic. Add it to the stock and salt to taste. Bring to a boil; add greens and simmer for 5 minutes. Beat eggs with cheese. Just before serving, pour the egg mixture gradually into the simmering soup, stirring until the egg sets. Do not let soup boil. Top with croutons.

MUSHROOM SOUP

6 servings

A simple soup, elegant enough for the finest dinner party.

2 Tbsp. olive oil
2 cloves garlic, chopped
1 lb. mushrooms, sliced
2 cups fresh tomatoes, chopped
3 cups chicken broth
1/2 tsp. salt
1/2 tsp. dried oregano
Salt and pepper, to taste
Grated Parmesan cheese (Optional)

Heat oil in a large saucepan. Sauté garlic and mushrooms for 5 minutes. Add remaining ingredients and bring to a boil. Cover and simmer 30 minutes. Add salt and pepper, to taste. Serve hot, sprinkled with grated Parmesan cheese, if desired.

MOM'S CHICKEN SOUP

8 servings

There's a wealth of health in this excellent version of Mom's traditional comfort food.

One 2-1/2 lb. chicken
2 qts. water
2 carrots, sliced
2 stalks celery, sliced
1 med. onion, chopped
3 cloves garlic, chopped
Salt and pepper, to taste
1 cup uncooked rice or noodles

The day before serving, simmer chicken, vegetables and spices in a large stock pot with the water and seasonings for 2 hours. Let cool and remove chicken and vegetables. Set aside. Refrigerate broth, covered, overnight. In the meantime, skin and de-bone the chicken. Keep 2 cups chopped chicken meat for the soup and use the rest for other purposes. Save the vegetables in a covered container and refrigerate. The next day, 30 minutes before serving, skim the fat off the top of the broth and return the liquid to a large sauce pot. Add the reserved chicken chunks, vegetables and rice. Simmer for 30 to 40 minutes. If using noodles, add to pot 10 to 15 minutes before serving.

NOTE: The vegetables can be puréed in a blender with a little broth and added to the soup before serving to make it thicker. Or, you can stir in a cup of light cream.

FRESH TOMATO SOUP

4 servings

Here's a great way to use your bumper crop of fresh tomatoes. This soup can be frozen for 2 months. You can also add 1 cup of rice to the mixture to make it even more hearty.

2 Tbsp. olive oil
1 med. onion, chopped
2 cloves garlic, chopped
1 carrot, chopped
1 stalk celery with leaves, chopped
4 cups chopped tomatoes
1 Tbsp. flour
2 cups water or chicken broth
2 Tbsp. fresh basil
Salt and freshly-ground pepper, to taste

Heat the oil in a large saucepan. Add the onion, garlic, carrot and celery. Sauté for 5 minutes until onion becomes transparent. Add tomatoes and simmer for 10 minutes, mashing occasionally with a wooden spoon until soft and pulpy. Sprinkle flour over the tomatoes and stir until smooth. Add water or broth and seasonings; bring to a boil and simmer, uncovered, for 20 minutes. Purée the soup in a blender or food processor, if desired. Reheat before serving.

SENATE BEAN SOUP

6 servings

The soup that won raves in the U.S. Senate cafeteria gets a garlicky lift with this adaptation.

1 lb. dried white beans
6 cups water, or more
1/2 tsp. crushed thyme
1 tsp. oregano
1/2 lb. potatoes
1/4 cup milk or light cream
1/2 cup chopped celery
1/2 cup chopped onion
2 cloves garlic, chopped
1/4 cup chopped fresh parsley
Salt and freshly-ground pepper, to taste

Soak beans in water overnight. Drain. Cover beans with 6 cups of fresh water and bring to a boil in a large saucepan. Cover and simmer over low heat for 1 hour. Scrub potatoes and cut into thick slices. Steam or microwave until tender. Mash and add milk or cream until fluffy. Add potatoes and remaining ingredients to cooked beans. Cover and simmer gently for another hour, stirring occasionally and lightly mashing beans with a fork or potato masher until soup becomes pulpy. Add more water, if needed. Taste for seasoning and serve warm.

MINESTRONE

6 servings

The Italians are famous for their frequent and flavorful use of garlic. This wonderful classic exemplifies how garlic adds that special touch of Italy to a meal-style soup. Don't be put off with the list of ingredients. Once you gather the goods, it's quite simple to put this soup together and well worth the effort.

2 cloves garlic, chopped
1 Tbsp. olive oil
1/2 cup chopped onion
6 cups water
1 - 6 oz. can tomato paste
1 - 16 oz. can tomatoes
2 cups cooked white or kidney beans
3 carrots, diced
2 stalks celery, sliced
1/2 lb. potatoes, diced
1 tsp. basil
1 tsp. oregano
1/4 cup chopped fresh parsley
1 cup uncooked pasta (shells, elbows, rotini or broken-up spaghetti)
2 cups shredded romaine or spinach
Salt and freshly-ground pepper, to taste
Grated parmesan cheese (Optional)

Sauté garlic briefly in oil over medium heat in a large stock pot or saucepan. Add the onion and cook for 5 minutes. Add the water, tomato paste, tomatoes, beans, carrots, celery and potatoes and simmer, covered, for 30 minutes. Add the remaining ingredients and cook for 30 minutes more. Serve with grated Parmesan cheese and hot, crusty Italian bread.

GAZPACHO

4 servings

This cold soup of Spanish origin is a delight on hot, summer evenings as a first course. Or add crusty bread and you have a terrific light meal. Plain, low-fat yogurt or the new non-fat sour cream makes an excellent garnish.

2 cups cold water or broth
1 lg. clove garlic, chopped
1 tsp. salt
4 Tbsp. olive oil
2 Tbsp. wine vinegar
4 cups fresh tomatoes, chopped
3 Tbsp. minced onion
1/2 tsp. (or more) hot pepper sauce, to taste
1 cup seasoned croutons, for garnish

Blend all ingredients, except croutons, in a blender or food processor fitted with a steel blade. Marinate in the refrigerator for 1 hour. Serve chilled, topped with croutons.

CABBAGE SOUP

6 servings

What can you say about a soup that combines the health-giving benefits of garlic with the anti-cancer fighter, cabbage? This delicious soup is hearty enough to serve as a complete meal in itself!

1 Tbsp. oil
1 Tbsp. butter
4 cloves garlic
1 lg. onion, chopped
4 cups shredded cabbage
6 cups chicken or vegetable stock
2 Tbsp. soy or tamari sauce
1 cup uncooked, long-grain rice
2 tsp. salt, if stock is unsalted
3/4 cup grated cheese, any mixture is fine

Heat oil and butter in a large saucepan or stock pot. Add split garlic to the pot. Add onion and sauté until limp, about 5 minutes. Add cabbage to pot and stir to coat with fat. Cook 5 minutes more. Add stock and soy sauce. Bring mixture to a boil. Add rice, season if necessary, and cover pot. Lower heat and simmer for 30 minutes. Serve with grated cheese.

YOGURT SOUP

4 servings

In the Middle East, this popular soup is often served with roast lamb or poultry. Fresh herbs really make a difference.

2 cups plain, low-fat yogurt
1/4 cup fresh mint or dill
1 cup peeled, seeded, shredded cucumber
1 clove garlic, crushed
1/4 cup fresh mint or dill, chopped
Salt and freshly-ground pepper, to taste

Beat all ingredients together with a wire whisk. Chill before serving. You can top each serving with a sprinkling of chopped nuts, if desired.

VICHYSSOISE

8 servings

This classic potato-based soup is both refreshing and filling.

2 Tbsp. olive oil or butter
1 cup chopped onion
1 cup sliced leeks
2 cloves garlic, crushed
5 cups diced potatoes
1 qt. chicken broth
Light cream (Optional)
Salt and freshly-ground pepper, to taste

Heat butter or oil in a large saucepan or stock pot. Sauté onion, leeks and garlic for 5 minutes or until soft. Add potatoes, broth and seasonings. Bring to a boil; cover and simmer for 25 minutes. Let cool. Purée soup in a blender or food processor. Chill and serve icy cold, blended with the additional cream just before serving. Season to taste.

Note: You can also make the soup hot on a winter's night.

SALADS

Garlic is a must in most any salad dressing. Here are some of my favorite salads. The dressings are adaptable to any mixture of vegetables.

COUNTRY BEAN SALAD

4 servings

An excellent main dish or accompaniment to a buffet.

Salad:

1 - 16 oz. can marinated three-bean salad, drained
1 - 15 oz. can chick peas, drained
1 - 16 oz. can white potatoes, drained
1/2 cup pickled beets, drained
2 cups salad greens, washed and shredded
1/4 cup crumbled bacon or bacon bits

Dressing:

1/2 cup olive oil
1/4 cup wine vinegar
3 cloves garlic, crushed
1 tsp. black pepper

Mix three bean salad with drained chick peas, potatoes and beets. Spoon over greens. Top with crumbled bacon. Thoroughly blend dressing ingredients. Drizzle dressing over all. Top with pepper.

GREEK COUNTRY SALAD

4 servings

I simply love this salad, not only because of my own Greek heritage but because it is the best main dish (or side salad) you can possibly have! Improvise, if you wish, by adding cooked shrimp, salmon or any other seafood. Serve with warm, crusty French, Greek, or Italian bread or pita pockets. Chill the dinner plates for an hour before serving.

Salad:

4 cups shredded mixed greens
1 red onion, sliced
1/2 cup sliced, pickled beets
1 tomato, chopped
1 cucumber, sliced thinly
1/2 lb. feta cheese, sliced
1 - 3-1/2 oz. jar marinated artichoke hearts (keep the marinade)
6 black Kalamata olives

Dressing:

1/2 cup extra virgin olive oil
4 cloves garlic, minced
1/4 cup wine vinegar
1 tsp. crushed oregano leaves
Salt & fresh ground pepper, to taste

Mix dressing (add the reserved artichoke oil) ingredients in a small jar and let stand. Arrange salad greens on a platter. Arrange the remaining salad ingredients over the greens. Drizzle dressing over all.

PASTA SALAD

4 servings

A great way to use leftover pasta. Spirals and shells work especially well in this main-dish salad that's also a good buffet dish with broiled chicken, roast beef or fish.

Salad:
2 cups cooked pasta
2 cups shredded salad greens
1 cup broccoli flowerets, lightly steamed
1 tomato, chopped
1/4 cup sliced black olives
1/4 cup sliced green olives
4 oz. shredded Cheddar cheese

Dressing:
1/2 cup olive oil
1/4 cup wine vinegar
1/2 cup low-fat yogurt
2 tsp. fresh minced garlic
1 tsp. black pepper
1 tsp. fresh minced dill
Salt and freshly-ground pepper, to taste

Combine dressing ingredients. Toss pasta with dressing, salt and pepper to taste. Let stand to develop flavors. Arrange tomatoes and broccoli on top of pasta mixture. Sprinkle with olives and cheese. Serve chilled on salad greens.

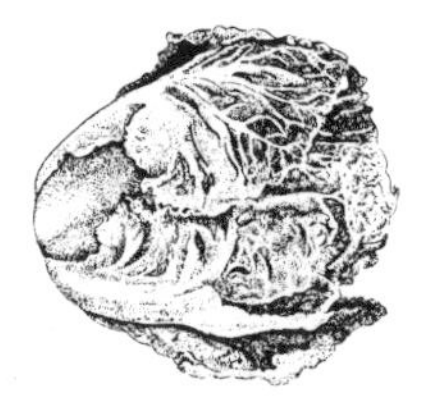

FISH SALAD

1 serving

Use canned, drained salmon, shrimp or tuna for this excellent dinner salad that's great on warm summer evenings or when you aren't hungry enough for a heavy meal. This recipe serves one heartily and can be increased to serve many more. The garlic gives extra zip to the salmon, important when you are using canned instead of fresh fish.

1 - 6 oz. can fish, drained
1 cup chopped celery
1/2 cup low-fat mayonnaise
1 clove garlic, crushed
1/2 cup finely-chopped onion or scallions
1/4 cup pimiento stuffed olives, chopped
1 tomato, sliced
1/3 cucumber, peeled and sliced
2 cups shredded salad greens
Freshly-ground pepper and paprika, to taste

Thoroughly combine fish, celery, mayonnaise, garlic, onion and olives. Arrange tomato and cucumber neatly on top of greens. Mound fish mixture in the center. Serve with sesame toast or pita bread.

CAESAR SALAD

4 servings

I don't know if Julius Caesar loved garlic, but this wonderful salad, that's a meal in itself, certainly gets its punch from lots of the bulb! I've left out the traditional raw egg for people with health concerns.

3 med. cloves garlic, crushed
1/4 tsp. dry mustard
1/4 tsp. salt
1/4 tsp. ground pepper
1/2 cup extra virgin olive oil
2 Tbsp. wine vinegar
1-1/2 tsp. Worcestershire sauce
8 anchovy fillets, drained and chopped
1 lg. head romaine lettuce, torn
1/2 cup grated Parmesan cheese
1-1/2 Tbsp. lemon juice
1 cup seasoned croutons

Combine the crushed garlic, mustard, salt, pepper, oil, vinegar, Worcestershire sauce and anchovies in a jar; cover and shake vigorously. Pour this dressing over the lettuce in a salad bowl. Add the cheese and toss the salad until it is well blended. Add the lemon juice and toss again. Add the croutons and toss gently; serve immediately.

SPINACH SALAD

4 servings

Another personal favorite!
This one gets its bite from lots of fresh garlic.

Salad:
1 lb. fresh spinach, washed and dried
1/2 cup bacon bits or fresh, crumbled cooked bacon
2 hard-boiled eggs, sliced
1/2 lb. mushrooms, washed and sliced thin
1/4 cup sliced beets
Seasoned croutons, to taste
1/4 cup crumbled blue cheese (Optional)

Dressing:
1/2 cup olive oil
5 cloves garlic, minced
1/4 cup wine vinegar
1 tsp. Dijon-style mustard
1 tsp. honey
Salt and freshly-ground pepper, to taste

Tear spinach greens in a shallow bowl. Top with neatly arranged bacon bits, egg slices, mushrooms, beets, croutons and blue cheese. Blend dressing ingredients well. Drizzle over salad.

POTATO BROCCOLI SALAD

4 servings

This is an easy way to make good use of tender new potatoes.

Salad:
2 lbs. steamed new potatoes
3 cups steamed broccoli flowerets
1/2 sm. red onion, sliced into rings
1 sm. red pepper, sliced into rings

Dressing:
3/4 cup olive oil
1/4 cup wine or cider vinegar
2 cloves garlic, peeled and minced
Salt and freshly-ground pepper, to taste

Halve the potatoes and place around the edges of a serving plate with the broccoli in the center. Chill until serving time. Arrange the slices of onion and pepper neatly over the potato and broccoli mixture when ready to serve. Combine the dressing ingredients in a small jar; shake well and pour over veggies.

CHRISTMAS SALAD

8 servings

This dish was a last-minute invention when we were invited to an unexpected holiday gathering. It was a festive hit!

Salad:
2 pts. cherry tomatoes, washed
2 - 10 oz. pkgs. fresh or frozen Brussels sprouts, cooked for 4 minutes or until barely tender
1/2 lb. feta cheese (or Mozzarella) cut into cubes
1/2 lb. olives, pimiento stuffed green or black

Dressing:
1/2 cup olive oil
2 Tbsp. wine vinegar
2 cloves garlic, minced
Freshly-ground black pepper, to taste

In an attractive serving bowl, combine tomatoes and sprouts. Top with chunks of feta and olives. Mix dressing ingredients well and drizzle over the salad. Top with a grinding of fresh pepper.

TABBOULEH

10 appetizer servings

This Middle Eastern dish is always a welcome addition to any buffet table.

Salad:
1 cup bulgur
1 cup tomato sauce
1 cup chicken broth
3 firm tomatoes, chopped
1 cup fresh parsley
1/2 cup chopped scallions

Dressing:
1/2 cup fresh lemon juice
2 Tbsp. olive oil
2 tsp. minced fresh garlic
Freshly ground pepper, to taste

Place the bulgur in a medium-sized casserole. Heat the tomato sauce and broth to boiling and pour the liquid over the bulgur, stirring once. Let stand for one hour. Mix bulgur with tomatoes, parsley and scallions.

Drain off excess liquid and chill bulgur until serving time. Mix dressing and pour over the bulgur. Toss well and let stand one hour before serving to let flavors blend. Bring to room temperature.

CARROT SALAD

4 servings

This is not your wimpy version of a mayonnaise-laced salad! It's a North African recipe that's spicy and delicious.

1 lb. fresh carrots, julienned
1/2 cup raisins
1/4 cup fresh lemon juice
1 tsp. olive oil
2 Tbsp. minced garlic
1 tsp. honey
1 tsp. cumin
1/4 cup chopped parsley
Freshly-ground black pepper, to taste

Place carrots in a bowl with the raisins and combine the remaining ingredients in a small jar or bowl. Pour the dressing over the carrots and raisins, tossing to mix well. Let stand one hour before serving.

VEGETABLES

Vegetables take on a new dimension when kissed with garlic. Ordinary green beans, for example, develop a subtle flavor that's quite remarkable. Stir-fried veggies are both healthy and tasty when sautéed in garlic-infused oil. Try some of these easy and garlicky vegetables for your family and friends. You'll be surprised how even diehard anti-vegetable eaters perk up when garlic adds its magic touch.

VEGETABLE STIR FRY

4 servings

Any combination of vegetables will taste good cooked this way. Just make sure to cut them into small pieces on a diagonal for maximum cooking surface.

1 cup each carrots, celery and zucchini, sliced on the diagonal
1/2 cup each broccoli and cauliflower flowerets
2 Tbsp. olive oil
3 cloves garlic, minced
1/4 cup dry white wine or chicken broth
1 Tbsp. soy or tamari sauce
1 Tbsp. lemon juice

Heat oil to 350° in a non-stick pan. Add vegetables and stir to coat with the oil. Add garlic and stir for 5 minutes. Add the remaining ingredients; stir and simmer the mixture, covered, for 2 minutes more, or until tender crisp.

GARLICKY CARROTS

4 servings

A simple but delicious dish that raises the lowly carrot to lofty elegance!

1 lb. carrots, sliced into 1-inch pieces
6 cloves fresh garlic, peeled and sliced
1/2 cup water
2 Tbsp. butter
Salt and freshly-ground pepper, to taste

Place carrots and garlic in a large saucepan. Add water and cook over medium heat covered, until just done, about 5 minutes. Add butter and seasonings; stir to melt and coat.

GREEK CAULIFLOWER

6 servings

This flavorful dish enhances any seafood or poultry dish.

- 1 head cauliflower
- 2 Tbsp. extra virgin olive oil
- 2 Tbsp. minced garlic
- 2 Tbsp. chopped parsley
- 1 Tbsp. lemon juice
- Salt and freshly-ground pepper, to taste

Separate cauliflower into flowerets and cook or steam just until tender. Heat the oil in a small frying pan and cook garlic and parsley for 2 minutes. Add lemon juice, salt and pepper to taste. Pour over the warm cauliflower and serve with additional chopped parsley, if desired.

STEAMED KALE WITH LEMON

Makes 4 servings

We love kale, now that we've found an easy and delicious way to prepare it. This iron-rich veggie is the perfect accompaniment with fish, chops or chicken. You can also use broccoli rabe, often called rappini, in this recipe.

- 1 lb. bunch kale, washed and coarsely chopped*
- 1 cup chopped onions
- 2 cloves garlic, chopped
- 4 Tbsp. olive oil
- Juice of one lemon
- Freshly-ground pepper, to taste

In a large non-stick saucepan (or one sprayed with Pam), heat the oil over medium heat for 2 minutes. Add the onion and garlic. Sauté for 5 minutes or until soft. Add the chopped kale. Stir well. Cover and lower the heat to low. Cook for 5 more minutes or until soft but still green. Add lemon and olive oil. Toss thoroughly. Heat 2 minutes more; season with pepper and serve.

*NOTE: If using broccoli rabe, chop the leaves and part of the stems, discarding the rough stems.

SAUTEED ZUCCHINI

This is the best way to make squash edible for males!

- 2 lbs. zucchini squash, sliced into 1/2-inch slices
- 1 onion, sliced
- 2 Tbsp. oil
- 2 cloves garlic, chopped
- 1 tsp. black pepper

In a large frying pan, heat the oil to sizzling on high heat. Add the zucchini, onion and garlic. Sauté for 4 minutes, stirring often. Add the pepper.

VARIATION: Add 1 chopped tomato.

FRIED MUSHROOMS

Makes 2 servings

We love all kinds of mushrooms! We sometimes find portabello slices on sale and that's a treat and a half! Serve with any broiled meat or rice and grain dish.

1 lb. sliced mushrooms
2 Tbsp. oil
1 Tbsp. garlic-parsley blend

Heat the oil in a non-stick frying pan. Add the mushrooms and sauté for 5 minutes, stirring often. Top with seasoning.

GARLIC MUSHROOMS

4 servings

A super-satisfying dish that couldn't be easier to make. Perfect for dinner parties.

1 lb. sliced mushrooms
4 Tbsp. olive oil
6 cloves fresh garlic, sliced
4 Tbsp. chopped fresh parsley
Salt and freshly-ground pepper, to taste

In a large skillet, sauté mushrooms in olive oil for 2 minutes. Add garlic, parsley, salt and pepper to taste. Simmer over medium heat, covered, 5 minutes more. Serve with roast chicken or lamb.

EGGPLANT WITH GARLIC

4 servings

Eggplant, that beautiful purple-hued vegetable, and garlic made a wonderful marriage of flavors! Here is a favorite dish that we prepare quite often.

1 eggplant, sliced into 1/2-inch slices
1 egg, beaten
2 cloves garlic, peeled and sliced thinly
1/2 cup olive oil
1 cup seasoned bread crumbs
1/4 cup grated Parmesan cheese

Pan Size: Rectangular casserole   Oven Temp.: 350°   Time: 15 minutes

Preheat oven. Dip eggplant slices, one at a time, in the beaten egg. Now coat with seasoned bread crumbs and lay flat on a platter. Refrigerate the coated slices for 1 hour. Meanwhile, prepare garlic. In a large frying pan, add the oil and heat just until smoking. Add the garlic and fry the eggplant slices over medium-high heat until brown on each side, about 5 minutes per side. Drain on paper towels.

Place the fried slices into an oiled, rectangular casserole. Arrange neatly and sprinkle with grated cheese. Bake for 15 minutes.

EGGPLANT STEW

4 servings

A quick version of ratatouille.

1/4 cup olive oil
1 eggplant, peeled and cubed
4 cloves garlic, chopped
1 onion, chopped
2 med. zucchini, sliced thinly
2 carrots, sliced thinly
2 cups chicken broth
2 cups tomato purée
2 tsp. dried oregano
Salt and freshly-ground pepper, to taste
1/4 cup wine vinegar

In a large saucepan, heat the oil and add eggplant cubes, garlic and onion. Sauté for 5 minutes, stirring frequently. Add the remaining ingredients, except the vinegar. Bring mixture to a boil; cover and simmer for 20 minutes. Stir in wine vinegar and adjust seasonings.

NOTE: You can add sliced, cooled potatoes, cooked and drained sausage or other varieties of green vegetables to the stew.

AMAZING BROCCOLI

I'm sure even former President George Bush, known for his dislike of broccoli, would adore this vitamin-rich vegetable prepared with a healthy dose of garlic! Serve cold with a garlic-laced mayonnaise or dip.

1 lb. fresh broccoli, cut into flowerets and stems
5 cloves garlic, crushed
1/2 cup water
1/4 cup wine vinegar
2 Tbsp. olive oil
1 tsp. salt

Place all ingredients in a large sauce pot. Bring to a boil, lower heat, cover and simmer until broccoli is just tender, about 5 minutes. Refrigerate several hours before serving.

BROCCOLI CASSEROLE

6 servings

An unusual way to prepare this popular vegetable that's sure to please even the most finicky eater.

1/2 cup chopped onion
1/4 cup olive oil
2 Tbsp. chopped garlic
1 lb. broccoli, steamed until tender and cut into 1" pieces
1 cup seasoned bread crumbs
1/2 cup grated Parmesan cheese
1 egg, beaten
Salt and freshly-ground pepper, to taste

Pan Size: Shallow casserole   Oven Temp.: 300°   Time: 20 minutes

Preheat oven. Sauté onion in the oil. Stir in garlic, broccoli, bread crumbs and cheese. Blend well. Add egg and blend again. Adjust seasoning to taste and place mixture into a shallow buttered casserole. Bake.

GARLIC GREEN BEANS

4 servings

Green beans are always plentiful and inexpensive. Here's an excellent way to make ordinary beans sizzle with flavor.

1 lb. green beans, washed, trimmed and cut into 2-inch pieces
2 Tbsp. butter
1 sm. onion, chopped
3 cloves garlic, minced
1 - 8 oz. can tomato sauce
1 tsp. dried oregano
Salt and freshly-ground pepper, to taste

Steam beans for 5 minutes until tender-crisp. Place in a serving dish and set aside. Fry onion and garlic in the butter in a small frying pan over medium heat for 3 minutes. Add tomato sauce and seasonings. Cook 5 minutes more. Pour over beans and toss thoroughly to blend flavors.

GARLIC SPUDS

4 servings

This unusual recipe is a sure-fire hit.

4 baking potatoes, peeled
1/2 tsp. salt
1/2 onion, sliced
4 cups water
3 cloves fresh garlic, peeled
1/2 cup light cream
2 Tbsp. butter or margarine
1/2 cup grated Cheddar cheese, for garnish

Boil potatoes, onion and garlic in salted water until soft. Drain off the water but reserve the onion and garlic. Mash the mixture with a fork or potato masher. Add light cream and butter; beat well. Sprinkle with grated cheese.

SPINACH CASSEROLE

6 servings

A tasty casserole that's great for company.

1 Tbsp. oil
2 lbs. fresh spinach
1 cup ricotta cheese
1 lb. cottage cheese
4 lg. eggs, well beaten
2 tsp. minced fresh garlic
1/2 tsp. nutmeg
Lots of fresh black pepper
1 Tbsp. lemon juice
Dash of paprika for the topping
1 cup fresh bread crumbs

Pan Size: 9x13 inch *Oven Temp.: 375°* *Time: 30 minutes*

Preheat oven. In a large skillet, heat oil and cook fresh spinach over medium heat, stirring until it wilts. Remove from heat and blend with remaining ingredients, except bread crumbs and paprika. Spread in a buttered pan; sprinkle with bread crumbs and paprika. Bake, covered, for 20 minutes; uncover and bake 10 minutes more.

TERRIFIC TOMATOES

"Simply irresistible" is how guests describe this colorful dish!

4 tomatoes, sliced
3 cloves garlic, minced
5 scallions, minced
2 Tbsp. chopped parsley
1/3 cup olive oil
1/4 cup wine vinegar
1 tsp. oregano
Salt and freshly-ground pepper, to taste

Arrange the tomatoes on a platter. Mix garlic, scallions and parsley; sprinkle over the tomatoes. Prepare dressing by mixing oil, vinegar and oregano. Drizzle over sliced tomatoes. Marinate 30 minutes before serving.

POTATO CURRY

6 servings

This adaptation of a Tibetan dish comes from my dear friend, Jacqueline Keeley, who worked and taught in Tibet for a decade.

4 lbs. unpeeled Idaho potatoes, cooked
1 cup chopped tomato
3 cloves garlic, minced
1/2 tsp. ginger
1/2 tsp. ground coriander
1/2 tsp. curry powder
2 Tbsp. olive oil
Salt and freshly-ground pepper, to taste

Peel cooled potatoes and cut them into 1/2-inch diced pieces. Put them into a glass serving bowl. In a blender, combine tomato, garlic, ginger, coriander, curry and olive oil. Blend well and toss with the potatoes. Season with salt and pepper. Serve at room temperature.

GARLIC PEAS AND RICE

6 servings

Use aromatic basmati rice for this flavorful dish.

1 tsp. olive oil
2 cloves garlic, minced
1 med. onion, chopped
1 tsp. curry powder
2 cups basmati rice
4 cups water
2 cups frozen peas
1 cup diced green pepper

Heat the oil in a large saucepan and add onion and garlic. Sauté for 5 minutes and add curry powder, rice and water. Bring to a boil and simmer, covered, for 40 minutes or until rice is tender. Add the peas and pepper and cook 5 minutes more.

CRUSTY POTATOES WITH GARLIC OIL

6 servings

This inexpensive but sumptuous dish may be simple fare, but to me and my family, it's delicious!

6 med. potatoes, peeled and sliced thinly
3 lg. onions, thinly sliced
4 garlic cloves, minced
1 - 28 oz. can plum tomatoes, drained and chopped
1/2 cup olive oil
2 tsp. oregano
Salt and freshly-ground pepper, to taste

Pan Size: Shallow baking dish *Oven Temp.: 400°* *Time: 70 minutes*

Preheat oven. In a large bowl, combine the potatoes, onions, garlic and tomatoes. Pour the olive oil and sprinkle oregano over the mixture and toss to coat well. Add salt and pepper to taste. Spread into baking dish and cover tightly with foil. Bake 30 minutes. Remove foil and bake 40 minutes longer, or until the potatoes are tender.

PASTA, GRAINS AND RICE

There is a growing awareness of the health benefits of pasta, grains and rice in our North American diet. Many experts believe that we eat too much animal protein with far too much fat. In this section, we feature a variety of low-fat, healthy recipes that rely on non-animal products to produce wonderful meals.

This first recipe, a quick version of ravioli and garlic with fresh vegetables, is an excellent example of how you can feed your family economically and in short order.

RAVIOLI WITH GARLIC-TOMATO SAUCE

4-6 servings

1 lb. fresh or frozen ravioli
1/4 cup olive or canola oil
3 garlic cloves, minced
3 med. peppers, cored and sliced into strips
1 - 10 oz. can stewed tomatoes
1 tsp. oregano
Freshly ground pepper, to taste
1/2 cup grated Parmesan cheese

Pan Size: 2-qt. casserole *Oven Temp.: 350°* *Time: Until heated*

Preheat oven. Bring a large pot of salted water to a boil and cook the ravioli for 10 minutes. Drain and place in a greased 2-quart casserole. In a large skillet, heat the oil over medium heat and add the garlic. Sauté for 2 minutes. Add the peppers and tomatoes; add the oregano and pepper. Simmer for 5 minutes. Pour sauce over ravioli. Sprinkle on the cheese and heat in the oven until serving time.

LOW-FAT MARINARA SAUCE

Makes 2-1/2 cups

1 Tbsp. olive oil
1 sm. onion, chopped fine
2 cloves garlic, chopped
1 green pepper, cored, seeded and chopped fine
1 tsp. oregano
1 tsp. black pepper
2 cups tomato sauce

Heat oil in a medium saucepan over low heat. Add onion and garlic and sauté for 5 minutes. Add remaining ingredients and simmer for 15 minutes. Serve over pasta, chicken or seafood.

NEW AGE CREAM SAUCE

Makes 2-1/2 cups

I love this sauce that I developed to use over cooked pasta, vegetables and just about anything I used to smother with cream sauce! It's even good over baked potatoes topped with cooked spinach.

2 Tbsp. butter
2 Tbsp. flour
2 Tbsp. minced garlic
2 cups chicken broth
1/2 cup skim milk
2 Tbsp. grated Parmesan cheese

In a small saucepan over low heat, melt butter. Stir in flour until smooth. Gradually add garlic and chicken broth, cooking over medium heat until the mixture starts to boil and becomes thick. Stir frequently to prevent lumps. When sauce is thick, lower heat and gradually add milk. Stir. Add cheese just before serving.

EGGPLANT SAUCE

Makes 3 cups

This is great for pasta, noodles, rice or polenta – that corn meal mixture that's a favorite in Italian cuisine. You can also use this sauce, with a little water or chicken broth added, to simmer chicken pieces into a wonderfully aromatic stew.

2 Tbsp. olive oil
3 garlic cloves, minced
1/2 tsp. red pepper flakes
1 - 28 oz. can tomato purée
2 tsp. red wine vinegar
1 med. eggplant, peeled and cubed
1 green pepper, cored, seeded and diced
2 cups sliced mushrooms
Salt and freshly-ground pepper, to taste

Heat the oil in a large skillet and sauté the garlic for a minute. Add red pepper flakes, tomato purée, vinegar, salt and pepper. Bring to a boil. Add the eggplant and simmer 10 minutes, stirring occasionally. Add the pepper and mushrooms and simmer 10 minutes more. Let cool and refrigerate overnight to develop flavors.

ANGEL HAIR PASTA WITH CLAMS

2 servings

Be careful not to overcook the pasta!

1 - 10 oz. jar whole clams
Reserved clam juice, plus enough water or white wine to make 1 cup
2 tsp. cornstarch
6 oz. angel hair pasta, also called capellini
1 Tbsp. olive oil
1 Tbsp. margarine
2 scallions, sliced
2 lg. garlic cloves, minced
Salt and freshly-ground pepper, to taste
1 tsp. oregano
3 Tbsp. chopped parsley

Drain the clams, reserving 1 cup juice. Add cornstarch to the juice with water or wine and blend well. Cook the capellini according to the package directions. Drain and reserve. Meanwhile, heat oil and margarine in a pan; add the scallions, garlic, salt and pepper. Cook for 3 minutes. Add oregano, clams and the clam-cornstarch mixture. Stir over low heat until mixture thickens. Add the parsley; turn up the heat and bring the sauce to a boil. Serve immediately over drained pasta.

EASY VEGETABLE LASAGNA

8 servings

A meatless variation of a popular favorite that is easily prepared in your microwave oven.

1 lb. mushrooms, sliced
1 lg. onion, chopped
4 cloves garlic, minced
1 lb. cottage cheese
1/2 lb. feta cheese, crumbled
1/2 cup grated Parmesan cheese
1 - 10 oz. pkg. frozen chopped spinach, defrosted and drained well
1 tsp. oregano
4 cups tomato or commercial spaghetti sauce
1 lb. lasagna noodles, cooked 10 minutes & drained
8 oz. shredded skim Mozzarella cheese

Pan Size: Microwavable lasagna pan *Temp.: HIGH* *Time: 8 minutes*
Temp.: MED. *Time: 30 minutes*

Combine mushrooms, onions and garlic in bowl. Cover and microwave for 3 minutes on HIGH. Combine cottage cheese, feta cheese, and half the Parmesan with the oregano in another bowl. In a microwavable lasagna pan, layer sauce, noodles, cheese mixture, spinach, mushrooms and onion mixture.. Repeat until all these ingredients are gone. Top with Mozzarella cheese. Cover with double plastic wrap. Refrigerate overnight.

Continued

Remove pan one hour before baking. Microwave on HIGH for 5 minutes. Microwave on MEDIUM 30 minutes more. Let stand 5 minutes before serving. Sprinkle remaining Parmesan over the casserole

NOTE: To cook conventionally, do not cover with plastic wrap. Bake, covered with foil, in a 350° oven for 60 minutes or until bubbly. Uncover for 15 more minutes.

PASTA PRIMAVERA

6 servings

Any variety of vegetables is great. Frozen vegetables make this an easy dish to make.

1 lb. pasta, such as shells, bows, rotini or elbows
1 Tbsp. oil
4 cloves fresh garlic, cut into slivers
Dash of salt
1 - 16 oz. pkg. frozen mixed Italian vegetables
2 cups New Age Cream Sauce (See page 172)
2 Tbsp. grated Parmesan cheese

Fill a large kettle or 5-quart saucepan with at least 2 quarts of water. Add a dash of salt and bring to a rolling boil. Add pasta and boil for 8 minutes. In the meantime, make New Age Cream Sauce and set aside. In a large skillet, sauté vegetables in hot oil for 5 minutes. Drain pasta and toss with vegetables. Pour new Age Cream Sauce over pasta and toss well. Sprinkle with grated cheese and serve immediately on warm dinner plates.

SHRIMP SCAMPI WITH PASTA

4 servings

A low-fat dish that combines sumptuous shrimp and pasta laced with garlicky flavor.

1 lb. fettucini
2 cups chicken broth
2 Tbsp. chopped garlic
2 Tbsp. chopped scallions
4 Tbsp. chopped parsley
1 lb. peeled, deveined shrimp
Salt and freshly-ground pepper, to taste
Parmesan cheese, to taste

Cook pasta according to package directions. Combine broth, garlic, scallions and parsley in a large saucepan. Bring to a boil and simmer, uncovered, 3 minutes. Add shrimp to broth. Simmer 5 minutes or until shrimp turns pink. Pour mixture over drained, warm pasta. Top with Parmesan cheese. Serve immediately.

PASTA WITH SAUSAGE

4 servings

A real Italian treat! Any pasta will do, but shells or noodles are great.

1/2 lb. pasta
2 tsp. olive oil
1/2 onion, sliced
4 cloves garlic, cut into slivers
1/2 lb. sliced mushrooms
1/2 lb. sliced sausage (turkey, veal or pork)
1 cup tomato or spaghetti sauce
1 tsp. salt
1 tsp. black pepper
1/2 cup grated Parmesan cheese

Heat 3 quarts water in a 5-quart saucepan. Heat oil in skillet. Add onions, garlic, mushrooms and sausage. Sauté 5 minutes. Add sauce, salt and pepper. Simmer 5 minutes more. When the water boils in the saucepan, add the pasta. Cook, uncovered, for 10 minutes. Drain the pasta in a colander. Place the pasta in a heated serving bowl. Toss with the sauce ingredients in the skillet, mixing well. Top with cheese and serve on warm dinner plates.

SUN-DRIED TOMATO ZITI

4 servings

The popularity of sun-dried tomatoes led me to create this vegetarian dish for my yoga buddies!

1 lb. ziti
1 cup oil-marinated sun-dried tomatoes
1 cup firm tofu, drained & crumbled
3 cloves garlic, chopped
4 Tbsp. fresh basil or 1 Tbsp. dried
2 Tbsp. balsamic vinegar
1 tsp.salt
1/2 tsp. white pepper
2 Tbsp. extra virgin olive oil
4 oz. jar marinated artichoke hearts, drained & chopped
2 Tbsp. minced fresh parsley
Parmesan cheese (can be soy) to taste

Cook ziti according to package directions until tender but still firm. Meanwhile, in a food processor, combine the tomatoes, tofu, garlic, basil, vinegar, salt, pepper and olive oil. Process until smooth.

Drain the pasta and toss with the sauce and artichokes. Sprinkle with parsley and cheese.

LOW-FAT NOODLES ALFREDO

4 servings

An updated version of a usually high-calorie, high-fat pasta dish.

1 lb. pasta
1/2 lb. low-fat, creamy cottage cheese
1 cup tomato sauce
1/4 cup grated Parmesan cheese
2 Tbsp. skim milk
2 cloves garlic, chopped
Salt and freshly-ground pepper, to taste
1 lg. ripe tomato, diced
1/4 cup chopped fresh basil leaves

Cook pasta according to package directions. Meanwhile, mix cottage cheese, tomato sauce, Parmesan cheese, milk, garlic, salt and pepper in the blender until smooth. Drain pasta and place in a warm serving casserole or skillet. Toss with cheese mixture and top with tomatoes and chopped basil.

PASTITSO - VEGETARIAN STYLE

I always thought my mother's version of this delicious Greek dish was a mite too heavy, so I experimented with lighter ingredients. This is really a winner! Serve it for a buffet dinner alongside roast turkey, pork or grilled chicken.

1 lb. elbows or ziti, boiled and drained
3 - 10 oz. pkgs. frozen chopped spinach, drained
16 oz. store bought or homemade garlic marinara sauce
1/4 cup butter
1/4 cup flour
1 qt. milk (can be low-fat)
4 eggs, beaten
1 cup Parmesan cheese

Pan Size: Lasagna pan *Oven Temp.: 350°* *Time: 40 minutes*

Preheat oven. Grease lasagna pan with Pam. Toss drained pasta with spinach and marinara sauce. In the meantime, melt butter in a medium saucepan over low heat. Stir in flour and blend until smooth; stir in milk, one cup at a time, stirring constantly over medium heat until thick. Pour one cup of the hot milk mixture into the beaten eggs. Add the egg-milk mixture into the saucepan and stir over medium low heat about 10 minutes. Add cheese and stir. Pour over pasta mixture and bake until top is golden brown. Let stand 1 hour before cutting into squares. Can be frozen and reheated in a 300° oven, loosely covered with foil for about 60 minutes or until piping hot.

STUFFED TOMATOES WITH COUSCOUS

4 servings

One of the best of the vegetarian cookbooks is Quick Vegetarian Pleasures by Jeanne Lemlin. Her collection of recipes is eclectic but easy to prepare. Here is a favorite summer dish that makes liberal use of fresh garlic. I've adapted Lemlin's recipe to trim time even further.

4 lg. ripe tomatoes
1 cup couscous
1-1/2 cups boiling chicken broth
1/2 cup oil or margarine
3 cloves garlic, minced
1 cup frozen peas, thawed
1 cup shredded Mozzarella cheese
1 tsp. dried oregano
Salt and freshly-ground pepper, to taste

Pan Size: Shallow glass pan *Oven Temp.: 375°Time: 30 minutes*

Preheat oven. Slice the top off the tomatoes and scoop out the insides. Reserve the pulp for another use. Turn over the tomatoes and let them drain on paper towels. Make the stuffing by pouring the chicken broth over the couscous and let stand, covered, for 10 minutes. Heat the oil in a frying pan and sauté the garlic and peas. Place the tomatoes in a shallow glass pan. When the garlic and peas are coated with oil, add them to the couscous along with the remaining ingredients. Fluff lightly with a fork and gently stuff the tomatoes with the couscous mixture. Bake, basting occasionally with the pan juices.

POULTRY

Garlic enhances any bird, adding a tantalizing aroma and a delicate taste. In the following recipes, you can interchange boneless, skinless chicken breast with turkey cutlets.

JIM'S TERIYAKI CHICKEN

Makes 4-6 servings

This is my husband's specialty – a low-cal standby that's good any time of the year, but especially during the hot summer months when nobody feels like cooking indoors. I prefer to use chicken breasts on the bone for this dish but, for economy's sake, I've called for a whole cut up chicken.

We often cook 8 chicken breasts on a Sunday and use them for easy standby meals during the week. For example, we'll have the following recipe one night, add cheese for a Chicken Parmesan or Paella the next night and make the Super Supper Salad the third night, adding romaine lettuce and hard-cooked eggs.

Extra chicken works well with just about anything, including cooked rice, packaged noodle mixes or roast potatoes.

This dish calls for nicely steamed spinach, carrots or any other vegetable. Cooked rice adds a final touch.

1 chicken, cut up, skin removed
2 cloves garlic, chopped
1 green onion, chopped
1/2 cup teriyaki sauce*
McCormick's Montreal steak spice**

Rub garlic into chicken. Sprinkle with green onion. Pour teriyaki marinade and steak spice over chicken. Cover tightly and refrigerate at least four hours. Broil on a greased outdoor grill or in the oven 5 inches from the heat source for 15 to 20 minutes, turning twice, or until there is no pink left in the juices when pierced with a fork.

*NOTE: For a really great homemade teriyaki sauce, mix 12 oz. of the lite commercial teriyaki sauce with a 1-inch piece of peeled ginger, 2 cloves peeled garlic and 1/4 cup cooking sherry in the blender. Whirl until the ginger and garlic are finely chopped. Save in a glass jar in the refrigerator. Marinate chicken, pork, fish or steak before broiling and you'll have such a treat!

**NOTE: McCormick's brand makes this spice. If you can't find it, use a lemon-pepper seasoning instead.

HONEY MUSTARD CHICKEN BREASTS

4 servings

This is a dish I truly treasure. It's delicious and very simple to prepare. Serve with steamed rice and spinach.

2 lbs. boneless, skinless chicken breasts
1/4 cup honey
2 Tbsp. prepared mustard
1 Tbsp. soy sauce
1 Tbsp. minced fresh garlic

Pan Size: Microwavable dish *Temp.: MED. HIGH* *Time: 15 minutes*

Mix honey, mustard, soy sauce and garlic. Pour over chicken breasts and cover tightly in a food storage bag or in a microwavable dish, covered with plastic wrap. Marinate in the refrigerator for several hours or overnight.

One hour before serving, remove the chicken from the fridge and let stand at room temperature. Microwave, covered with vented plastic wrap, for 15 minutes on MEDIUM HIGH, turning twice. Cook until done.

NOTE: You can also fry the chicken breasts in a non-stick pan for 10 minutes on each side or roast in a 350° oven for 30-34 minutes.

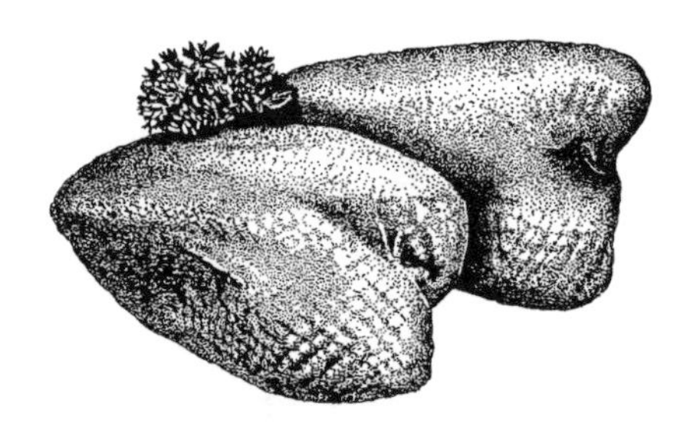

BREADED CHICKEN CUTLETS WITH CHEESE

4 servings

This lovely, easy dish is delicious with steamed Brussels sprouts or broccoli, cooked with fresh garlic, of course!

4 chicken cutlets
2 Tbsp. seasoned flour or bread crumbs
1 Tbsp. margarine or olive oil
4 slices Mozzarella cheese
1 tsp. garlic powder or granulated garlic

Dip the chicken breasts in bread crumbs or flour to cover. Heat oil or margarine in a large skillet and brown breasts on both sides, about 4 minutes each side. Top with slices of cheese and sprinkle with garlic. Lower heat, and simmer 10 minutes more. Serve over hot noodles.

NOTE: The Mozzarella can be omitted or replaced with 1/2 cup grated Parmesan cheese.

LEMON HERB CHICKEN

4 servings

You can easily double, triple or even quadruple this recipe!

4 chicken leg quarters,
skin removed
1 Tbsp. olive oil
1 Tbsp. fresh lemon juice
1 tsp. oregano
1 clove garlic, minced

Pan Size: Casserole *Oven Temp.: 350°* *Time: 20 to 30 minutes*

Mix olive oil and lemon juice, oregano and garlic for the marinade. Pour marinade over chicken; cover with plastic wrap and chill for at least 2 hours, turning chicken over twice. Preheat oven. Place leg quarters in a casserole large enough to hold them in a single layer and bake 20 to 30 minutes, turning the legs over once.

Note: Pierce chicken with a fork and if the juice runs clear, they are cooked.

CHINESE CHICKEN BREASTS

4 servings

An easy dish that tastes exotic.

1 tsp. sesame oil
2 whole boneless, skinless
chicken breasts
2 cloves garlic, minced
1/4 cup chopped onion
2 cups broccoli flowerets
1 - 10 oz. pkg. frozen snow pea pods
(fresh are even better)
1/4 cup soy sauce
1/2 cup dry white wine

Heat the oil in a large skillet. Add chicken breasts and brown on both sides. Add garlic, onion, broccoli, snow pea pods, soy sauce and wine; stir. Cover and simmer for 10 minutes. Serve over steamed rice.

ROAST CHICKEN

4 servings

Adding slivers of fresh garlic to any roast elevates a simple meal to one fit for a king – or queen! Use a sharp knife and cut holes all over the bird. Then, insert slivers of fresh garlic into the slits.

1 - 3 lb. roasting chicken
2 whole garlic cloves, cut into thin slivers
Salt and freshly-ground pepper, to taste
2 med. potatoes, cut into quarters
4 carrots, cut into 1-inch pieces
1 onion, cut into quarters
1/4 cup water or wine

Pan Size: Baking dish *Oven Temp.: 350°* *Time: 1 hour*

Preheat oven. Clean the chicken under running water. Trim away all excess fat. Make small slits in the chicken skin. Insert garlic into slits. Sprinkle seasoning over the bird.

Surround the chicken with vegetables in baking dish. Add 1/4 cup wine or water. Cover loosely with foil and cook for 45 minutes. Remove foil and cook 15 minutes longer or until the bird is browned and the veggies are tender-crisp.

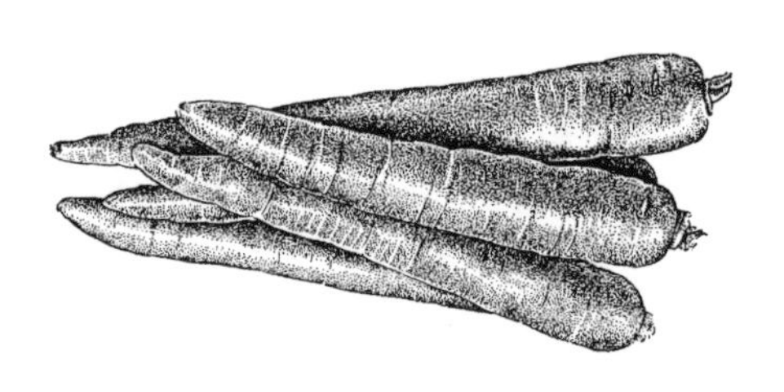

CURRIED CHICKEN

4 servings

This dish has an Indian heritage and a very special exotic flavor. It is delicious served with brown or white rice.

3 lb. chicken, skinned and cut into serving pieces
1 cup plain non-fat yogurt
3 cloves garlic, crushed
1 tsp. curry powder
2 Tbsp. oil

Pan Size: Non-stick electric skillet *Temp.: 400°* *Time: 45 minutes*

Place the chicken pieces in a bowl. In another smaller bowl, combine the yogurt, curry and garlic. Toss the chicken with the yogurt mixture and coat well. Cover the bowl and refrigerate overnight.

Remove chicken pieces from marinade. Heat oil in an electric skillet at 400°. Brown chicken well on all sides. Add reserved marinade to skillet. Stir and cover. Reduce heat and simmer for 30 minutes.

MOCK CHICKEN CACCIATORE

4 servings

This is a streamlined version of one of my all-time favorite dishes. I used to prepare it with whole, cut-up chicken –with the skin left on! Here's an up-to-date version to fit today's health conscious and busy lifestyle.

2 tsp. oil for frying
2 cloves garlic, chopped
1 cup chopped onion
4 skinless chicken breast halves, with bone
1 lb. sliced mushrooms
1 - 16 oz. can stewed tomatoes
1 tsp. oregano
Salt and freshly-ground pepper, to taste

Preheat an electric skillet to 350°. Heat oil in skillet; add garlic and onion. Add chicken breasts and brown on each side. Add mushrooms. Stir for 3 minutes. Add tomatoes and spices. Cover the skillet and cook for 20 more minutes. Serve over hot, cooked noodles or with French or Cuban bread.

GRILLED CHICKEN AND EGGPLANT PARMESAN

Makes 8 servings

This dish came to me from The Lunas Ristorante, in Delray Beach, Florida. It's infinitely lighter and tastier than the traditionally fried version, to my mind. This also makes an excellent dish to serve for a crowd. Adjust the ingredients accordingly. I make each of the eggplant and chicken dishes separately in 9x13 inch pans when I do this for a crowd. Accompany with boiled ziti tossed with chicken broth, minced garlic and oregano, warm crusty rolls and a good Caesar salad.

8 chicken breasts, skinless and, boneless, pounded until they are even
2 Tbsp. complete herb seasoning
1 tsp. freshly-ground black pepper
2 lg. eggplants
4 cups tomato sauce or purée
1 Tbsp. minced garlic
1 lb. fresh low-fat Mozzarella
1/2 cup grated non-fat Parmesan cheese

Pan Size: 2 - 9x13 inch *Oven Temp.: 300°* *Time: 20 minutes*

Have ready casserole dishes, preferably stainless steel. In the morning, marinate the breasts in zipper lock bags with the herb seasoning and black pepper. Refrigerate, turning once or twice.

One hour before serving, slice the eggplants and salt each slice lightly. Place, stacked, in a large dish. Heat the broiler or outdoor grill. Remove the

Continued

chicken from the fridge and grill, about 10 minutes each side.

In the meantime, mix the tomato sauce or purée with the garlic and place 2 cups in each of the pans. Preheat the oven. When the chicken is done, place the breasts neatly in one of the pans and now grill the eggplant for about 5 minutes on each side or until they are brown.

Place the eggplant in the other casserole. Slice the Mozzarella thinly and top the chicken and eggplant. Repeat with the Parmesan. Cover each casserole loosely with foil and place in the oven. Heat for 20 minutes.

At this point, boil the water for your pasta. I make 1-1/2 lbs. of ziti. Cook according to directions on package. Drain and toss with your choice of sauce.

CHICKEN AND SWEET POTATO DINNER

Makes 4 servings

This healthy, vitamin-rich meal takes almost no time to prepare. Chicken thighs are a great bargain and often come already boned and skinned. You can also use leftover grilled chicken for this economical dish that's chock full of vitamins.

4 chicken legs, or 8 thighs, skin removed
1/4 cup barbecue sauce
2 Tbsp. minced garlic
2 sweet potatoes, scrubbed and cut into thin sticks
1/4 cup canola oil

Pan Size: Cookie sheet *Oven Temp.: 400°* *Time: 45 minutes*

Preheat oven. Spray a cookie sheet or shallow pan with vegetable spray. Toss chicken with barbecue sauce and garlic. Toss potatoes with the oil. Place the chicken and potato slices on the cookie sheet and bake, uncovered, for 30 minutes, turning chicken once and stirring potatoes once. Bake until potatoes and chicken are cooked through, about 45 minutes.

TURKEY CUTLETS FRANÇAISE

4 to 5 servings

A super dish from my dear friend, Roz Suss, who also believes that flavorful food need not be time consuming nor fattening.

2 eggs, beaten
Salt and pepper
2-1/2 lbs. turkey cutlets, pounded thin
1/2 cup flour
1/4 cup oil
2 cloves garlic, peeled and sliced
6 Tbsp. butter
Juice of 1/2 lemon
1 cup chicken broth
1/4 cup white wine

Mix salt and pepper into beaten eggs. Dip cutlets into the flour, then into the egg, then back into the flour. Set aside. Heat oil in a 12-inch non-stick skillet. Add the garlic slices. Fry the cutlets on both sides until brown. Drain well on paper towels. Sauté for 2 minutes. Clean skillet and add butter; melt over low heat.

Add lemon, broth and wine and return cutlets to skillet. Simmer for 15 minutes, covered. Sprinkle with parsley before serving.

TURKEY DIVAN

4 servings

An excellent way to use leftover turkey – or chicken.

8 slices cooked turkey or 2 cups leftover chopped turkey
2 - 10 oz. pkgs. frozen broccoli spears, thawed
1 - 10 oz. can cream of mushroom soup
1 soup can low-fat milk
1 tsp. minced garlic
1 tsp. white pepper
1/2 cup shredded Swiss or Mozzarella cheese
Hot, cooked rice or noodles

Pan Size: Shallow casserole *Oven Temp.: 350°* *Time: 45 minutes*

Preheat oven. Place turkey in a shallow casserole. Top with broccoli spears. Mix soup and milk; pour over casserole. Sprinkle on spices. Bake, covered, for 30 minutes. Top with shredded cheese and heat 15 minutes more, uncovered. Serve with rice or noodles.

ROAST TURKEY OR TURKEY BREAST

Prepare the same way as you would roast chicken (page 180), but adjust cooking times to the size of your bird. Allow 20 minutes per pound in a conventional oven and 10 to 12 minutes per pound in the microwave. Remember to turn the bird over halfway through for even cooking.

TURKEY JAMBALAYA

4 Servings

Garlic gives this easy but elegant dish extra richness and flavor.

2 tsp. sesame oil
4 cloves garlic, peeled and cut in halves
1 lb. turkey cutlets, cut into strips
1 onion, chopped
1 green pepper, chopped
1/2 cup chopped celery
1/2 lb. turkey sausage, chopped
1-1/2 cups long-grain rice
2 cups chicken broth
1 cup tomato sauce or tomato purée
1/2 lb. frozen shrimp
1 - 10 oz. pkg. frozen peas
1/2 lb. mushrooms, sliced
Salt and freshly-ground pepper, to taste
1 tsp. paprika

Pan Size: Electric skillet *Temp.: 350°* *Time: 3 to 5 minutes*
Temp.: 300° *Time: 20 minutes*

Preheat skillet. Add oil; when it sizzles add garlic halves, turkey cutlets, onion, green pepper, celery, sausage and rice. Stir and cook for 3 to 5 minutes. Add the broth and tomato sauce. Cover and reduce heat to 300°. Cook for 15 minutes or until almost all of the liquid is absorbed. Add the remaining ingredients. Stir and cook 5 minutes longer, adding more broth, if necessary.

TURKEY CHILI AND MACARONI

4-6 servings

A new slant on an old favorite!

1 lb. ground turkey
1 - 16 oz. can stewed tomatoes
1 cup chopped onion
3 cloves garlic, minced
1 tsp. chili powder
1 tsp. oregano
Freshly-ground pepper, to taste
1 - 16 oz. can kidney beans, drained and rinsed
2 cups frozen mixed vegetables, thawed
1/2 lb. elbow macaroni, cooked al dente and drained

Put turkey into a large, non-stick frying pan or electric skillet. Cook, stirring, over medium heat until all traces of pink disappear. Add tomatoes, tomato sauce, onion, garlic and seasonings. Simmer, covered, for 20 minutes.

Add the beans and vegetables. Simmer, covered, 10 minutes more. Add the cooked macaroni and heat thoroughly before serving. Serve with a mixed green salad and rolls.

MEAT AND EGG DISHES

Be creative in preparing even plain, broiled steaks and chops. Buy cuts that look lean and then trim excess visible fat before cooking. Let garlic – not unhealthy fat – add the flavor.

TENNESSEE CHILI

6-8 servings

2 Tbsp. vegetable oil
2 cloves garlic, minced
1 lg. onion, chopped
1 lb. lean ground beef
2 Tbsp. chili powder
1/2 tsp. salt
1 - 28 oz. can whole tomatoes
2 - 28 oz. cans kidney beans, drained and rinsed
Chopped scallions
Grated Cheddar cheese
Chopped fresh tomatoes

Heat oil in a 3-quart saucepan over medium-high heat. Add garlic and onion and cook 3 minutes, stirring frequently. Add ground beef and cook, stirring, until the meat loses its pink color. Stir in spices. Add tomatoes with their liquid and bring to a boil, stirring and breaking up the tomatoes with the back of a spoon.

Reduce heat to low and cook uncovered 20 minutes or until mixture thickens, stirring occasionally. Add beans, stir and heat for 3 minutes longer. Serve with chopped scallions, grated Cheddar cheese and chopped, fresh tomatoes for garnish.

FRITTATA

Makes 4 servings

This is very much like an omelet, except you bake the eggs in the oven.

2 Tbsp. butter
1/2 cup chopped onion
1 tsp. minced garlic
1/4 cup chopped green pepper
1 lg. potato, sliced thinly
8 eggs, beaten
1 cup marinara sauce
1 cup shredded low-fat cheese of your choice
Salt and freshly-ground pepper, to taste

Pan Size: Oven-proof skillet *Oven Temp.: 350°* *Time: 30 minutes*

Preheat oven. In an oven-proof skillet, heat the butter until it sizzles over medium heat. Add the onion, garlic and potato. Sauté for 5 minutes, or until all ingredients are golden. Pour the eggs over the mixture. Pour the marinara sauce evenly over the eggs. Top with cheese and spices. Bake for 20 - 30 minutes until eggs are set and the potatoes are tender.

STEAK WITH MUSHROOMS

Makes 4 servings

Now we're talking a man's meal! But lean sirloin steak can be a healthy meal if you trim off excess fat and grill the meat well. Add steamed broccoli and a salad.

2 lb. piece of sirloin steak, trimmed of excess fat
1/4 cup teriyaki sauce
1 tsp. steak sauce
2 tsp. black pepper
2 tsp. minced garlic
1 lb. sliced mushrooms

Marinate the steak in a zipper lock bag with the teriyaki sauce, steak sauce and spices for two days. Heat the grill or broiler for 5 minutes on high. Grill or broil the steak for 5 minutes each side. In the meantime, sauté the mushrooms in a non-stick pan over high heat until brown. Top the steak with the mushrooms and serve.

RUMP ROAST

8 servings

This lean cut can be easily prepared – if you are patient. To serve, slice thinly against the grain.

1 - 5 lb. rump roast
1 - 1 oz. pkg. onion soup mix
2 Tbsp. minced fresh garlic
1/2 cup ketchup
1 cup red wine or water
1 onion, quartered
4 carrots, scraped and left whole
4 sm. red potatoes, washed and scrubbed

Pan Size: Lg. casserole or roasting pan
Oven Temp.: 325° *Time: 2 hours*

Preheat oven. Place the roast in a large casserole or roasting pan. Sprinkle with soup mix, garlic and ketchup. Pour wine or water over the roast. Cover with foil wrap. Cook for 1 hour. Add carrots, onions and potatoes; cover and cook 30 minutes more. Uncover, and roast for another 1/2 hour. Let stand 15 minutes before carving and serving.

BEEF POT ROAST

12 servings

Here's a hearty dinner that's chock full of low-fat goodness. Make this when you want to warm the soul and spirit!

8 cloves garlic
3 Tbsp. wine vinegar
10 black peppercorns
1 Tbsp. oregano
3 cups water
2 slices bacon, sliced crosswise into 1/4-inch pieces
1 - 4 lb. rump roast

Pan Size: Casserole *Oven Temp.: 325°* *Time: 2-1/2 hours*

Preheat oven. Combine garlic, vinegar, peppercorns, oregano and water in a blender or food processor. Process until smooth, about 1 minute. Heat bacon in a flame-proof casserole until it begins to smoke. Add the roast and brown all over. Pour garlic mixture over the roast and cover with foil. Bake for about 1-1/2 hours. Turn the meat over; baste with the sauce and cover again. Roast for another hour or until the meat is very tender when pierced with a fork. Cool slightly and serve sliced thin with the sauce spooned over each piece.

MOIST MEAT LOAF

2-4 servings

A great microwave meal that's ready in minutes!

1-1/2 lbs. lean ground round or chuck
2 Tbsp. minced, fresh garlic
2 med. onions, finely chopped
1/2 cup rolled oats
1 egg, beaten
2 Tbsp. chopped fresh parsley
Salt and freshly-ground pepper, to taste
1/4 cup ketchup

Pan Size: 10-inch plate *Temp.: HIGH* *Time: 16 minutes*
Temp.: MED. *Time: 5 minutes*

Place the meat on a 10-inch microwavable plate or casserole. Make a well in the center and add garlic, onions, oats, egg, parsley, salt and pepper. Pour in the ketchup. Mix well with your hands and form into an oval in the center of the dish. Pour the rest of the tomato sauce down the center.

Microwave, uncovered, on HIGH for 16 minutes, rotating the dish twice. Microwave 5 minutes more on MEDIUM and let stand 5 minutes before serving. Cut into slices and serve with steamed broccoli or spinach and a green salad.

ROAST LAMB

10 servings

A great roast that your family and guests will adore.

1 - 5 lb. leg of lamb, trimmed of all visible fat
5 cloves of garlic, cut into slivers
2 Tbsp. dried oregano
1/4 cup lemon juice
1/2 cup white wine

Pan Size: Roasting pan *Oven Temp.: 325°* *Time: 1-1/2 hours*

Preheat oven. Wipe roast well with a damp paper towel and with a very sharp, small knife, cut about 20 holes into it. Insert a garlic sliver into each hole. Mix lemon juice and oregano and rub it over the lamb with your fingers. Place in a roasting pan and pour the wine into the pan. Cook, uncovered, for about 1-1/2 hours, basting every 20 minutes with the pan juices. Let stand 15 minutes before carving.

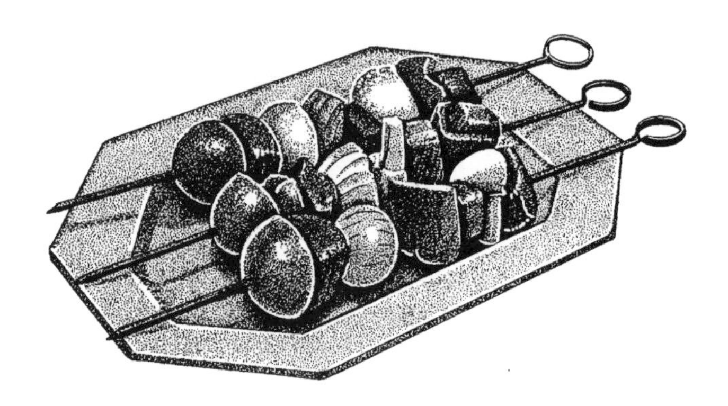

SUCCULENT SKEWERS

4 servings

A wonderful dish for company or family.

1 lb. top round beef, cut into 1-inch cubes
1/2 cup olive oil
1/4 cup red wine vinegar
2 cloves garlic, crushed
2 tomatoes, quartered
2 green peppers, cut into 1-inch chunks
1 lg. onion, quartered and separated
1/2 lb. mushroom caps

Marinate the beef cubes in the dressing, combining the oil, vinegar and garlic overnight. Thread them onto metal skewers, saving the marinade, alternating with the vegetables. (I like to cover each beef cube with an onion piece, then a tomato, green pepper and mushroom cap.) Broil 5 inches from the heat source for 5 minutes on each side or grill on an outdoor barbecue for the same length of time. Baste with leftover marinade. Serve with rice.

PORK CHOPS

2 servings

This was one of the first dishes I ever made! It still is one of the tastiest, cheapest and simplest main-dish meals you can prepare.

2 Tbsp. oil
4 pork chops, trimmed of visible fat
1/2 cup long-grain rice
2 cloves garlic, chopped
1/4 cup chopped onion
1-1/2 cups chicken broth
1 green pepper, cored, seeded and chopped
1 tomato, sliced
Salt and freshly-ground pepper, to taste

Pan Size: Electric skillet *Temp.: 350°* *Time: 15 minutes*
Temp.: 275° *Time: 20 minutes*

Preheat an electric skillet to 350°. Add the oil. Brown the pork chops for 5 minutes on each side. Remove and place on a plate. Add rice, garlic and onions to the skillet. Stir until lightly brown, about 5 minutes. Add chicken broth and stir. Place the reserved pork chops over the rice mixture and top with green pepper and tomato slices. Cover skillet and cook for 20 minutes at 275° or until all liquid is absorbed.

BEEF STEW

Makes 6 servings

Ah! Who wouldn't love a big pot of steamy stew on a cold winter's night! Use beef, lamb or pork for this stew.

1-1/2 lbs. stew meat
2 Tbsp. oil
1/4 cup powdered gravy mix or flour
4 cloves garlic
2 onions, chopped
6 carrots, peeled and sliced into 1-inch pieces
6 celery stalks, cut into 1-inch pieces
4 med. potatoes, peeled and cut into 1-inch sections
2 turnips, peeled and cut into 1-inch pieces
2 - 10 oz. cans beef broth
1 - 16 oz. can peeled tomatoes and juice
Salt and pepper, to taste

Pan Size: Lg. stock pot *Oven Temp.: 350°* *Time: 1 hour*

Preheat oven. In a large stock pot, about 3 quarts, heat the oil over medium heat. Add the meat, garlic, onions and gravy mix or flour. Stir until the meat is brown. Add the remaining ingredients. Stir and bring to a boil, uncovered. Cover and place in the oven for 1 hour. Serve with hot French bread and a salad.

NOTE: You can also put all the ingredients into a crock pot and simmer on low all day while you are at work. Boy, what a welcome you'll get when you return!

VARIATION: Sliced mushrooms can be added 10 minutes before serving.

SHEPHERD'S PIE

Makes 8 servings

This is my husband's favorite dish! It's surprisingly easy to prepare and makes a great Sunday night supper with leftovers for Monday.

2 lbs. potatoes, peeled and chopped
1/2 cup milk
1 Tbsp. butter
2 lbs. ground turkey or beef or a combination of both
1 onion, chopped
3 cloves garlic, chopped
1 env. onion soup mix
1 Tbsp. brown gravy mix
1/2 cup water
1 tsp. Worcestershire sauce
1 Tbsp. steak sauce
1/4 cup ketchup
Black pepper, to taste
1 - 14 oz. can corn, drained
1 cup frozen peas (no need to defrost) (Optional)
1 cup chopped fresh mushrooms (Optional)
1 cup shredded Mozzarella cheese
1 tsp. freshly-ground pepper

Pan Size: 2-qt. casserole *Oven Temp.: 350°* *Time: 20 minutes*

Boil the potatoes in salted water; drain most of the liquid, saving about 1 cup. Mash with milk and butter and set aside. In a large non-stick frying pan over medium high heat, brown the meat, onions and garlic, stirring to break up lumps. Drain off fat.

Mix the gravy mix with water, onion soup mix, Worcestershire sauce and steak sauce. Add ketchup, black pepper, corn, peas and mushrooms (if using) and stir into the meat mixture. Reduce heat to low and simmer for 10 minutes, stirring often.

Preheat oven. Transfer the meat mixture into casserole. Top with mashed potatoes and sprinkle on the cheese and ground pepper. Bake 20 minutes until slightly brown. Turn off the oven and serve warm.

NOTE: This dish can also be frozen. Heat in a 300° oven, uncovered, until bubbly, about 30 minutes.

VARIATION: Grated Cheddar may be substituted for Mozzarella cheese.

APPLESAUCE ROAST PORK

5-6 servings

A wonderful company dinner!

1 - 3 lb. pork rib roast
3 cloves garlic, minced
1 onion, sliced
1 tsp. oregano
1 cup unsweetened applesauce
2 tsp. cinnamon
Salt and freshly-ground pepper, to taste

Pan Size: Roasting pan *Oven Temp.: 350°* *Time: 1 hour*

Preheat oven. Place pork roast in a pan. Cover with garlic, onion slices and spices. Refrigerate 4 hours, covered, before roasting. Roast, uncovered, for 1 hour. Let stand 15 minutes before carving. Serve with applesauce sprinkled with cinnamon.

LEFTOVER PAELLA

Makes 2 servings

An easy dish that's adaptable for many leftovers or even shrimp!

Vegetable spray
1 onion, chopped
2 cloves garlic, chopped
1 green pepper, chopped
1 cup instant brown rice
2 cups water
2 tsp. chicken bouillon
2 Tbsp. teriyaki sauce
2 cups sliced leftover meat or chicken
1 - 10 oz. pkg. spinach, thawed

Heat a non-stick frying pan to 350° or higher; add vegetable spray. Sauté onion, garlic, pepper and rice for 3 minutes, stirring. Add water, chicken bouillon and teriyaki sauce. Cover and cook for 15 minutes. Lower heat to simmer; add chicken and spinach. Cook, covered, for 10 minutes more or until all the liquid is absorbed. Serve on heated plates.

BARBECUED RIBS

Makes 4 servings

A super way to begin a barbecued meal! Get the leanest ribs you can find for this dish. It's also a good main dish meal served with corn on the cob and a salad.

4 lbs. pork or beef ribs
1/2 cup ketchup
1 cup barbecue sauce
1 Tbsp. Worcestershire sauce
 or steak sauce
2 tsp. minced garlic
Freshly ground black pepper,
 to taste

Pan Size: Microwave dish *Temp.: MED.* *Time: 20 minutes*

Boil ribs in salted water until tender, about 1 hour. Mix the remaining ingredients and brush over the ribs. Cover tightly and marinate for at least 8 hours. Grill or broil over medium heat until brown, about 10 minutes per side.

BAKED HAM WITH PINEAPPLE

8-9 servings

A cooked ham will go a long way. Bake it on Sunday and you'll have leftovers for the week. Slice it for omelets and sandwiches. Or chop it to use in rice and pasta dishes.

Serve with roasted potatoes and Garlic Green Beans or Garlicky Carrots.

1 - 5 lb. fully-cooked ham,
 trimmed of all visible fat
15 whole cloves
3 cloves garlic, peeled
1 - 10 oz. can pineapple chunks
 or slices
1 sm. jar maraschino cherries
 for garnish, if desired

Pan Size: Roasting pan *Oven Temp.: 300°* *Time: 1 hour*

Preheat oven. Place the ham in a roasting pan or baking dish. Cut the surface into diamond shapes with a sharp knife and place a whole clove in each intersection. Mince the garlic. Drain the pineapple slices and reserve the juice. Combine the garlic and juice and spoon over the ham. Place the pineapple over and around the ham. Roast, uncovered, for 1 hour, basting the ham with pan juices every 15 minutes or so. Remove to a platter to carve and surround with pineapple and cherries.

SEAFOOD

If garlic and poultry are a marriage made in gourmet heaven, then garlic teamed with fish must rank as the ultimate union!

GARLIC CATFISH FILLETS

4 servings

Farm-raised catfish is healthful and almost pollution-free. These fillets are fast and easy to make.

2 lbs. catfish fillets
1 egg, beaten
1 Tbsp. Worcestershire sauce
1 cup cornmeal
Salt and freshly-ground white pepper, to taste
2 Tbsp. butter or margarine
4 cloves garlic, peeled and left whole
2 Tbsp. oil

Dip fillets in the beaten egg mixed with Worcestershire sauce and dredge in cornmeal. Lay in a single layer on waxed paper. Meanwhile, heat the oil and butter in a large skillet. Add the cloves of garlic and stir to blend the flavors. Add the fillets and brown for 3 minutes on each side or until the fish flakes easily with a fork. Serve with lemon wedges and sprinkle with white pepper.

FAMOUS GREEK FISH FILLETS

4-6 servings

This easy and delicious recipe is sure to become a family favorite – even with those who say they hate fish. Serve the fillets over steamed brown rice and accompany with sliced Greek or Italian bread.

It's an ideal dish if you don't have access to a fish market. The tomato sauce cuts the "frozen" taste of the fish.

2 lbs. fresh or frozen fish fillets
2 cloves garlic, chopped
1 med. onion, sliced
1 green pepper, cored, seeded and sliced
1 carrot, thinly sliced
2 cups tomato sauce
1/2 cup chicken broth or white wine
1 tsp. oregano
1 tsp. white pepper
1/4 cup olive oil

Pan Size: 9x13 inch *Oven Temp.: 350°* *Time: 30 minutes*

Preheat oven. Place fish fillets neatly along the bottom of pan. Cover evenly with vegetables and garlic. Blend tomato sauce with chicken broth or wine and pour over the fillets. Sprinkle with seasonings. Drizzle olive oil over the top. Bake, uncovered, for 30 minutes.

MOROCCAN CATFISH COUSCOUS

4-6 Servings

We have learned to love couscous, a semolina cereal indigenous to Morocco and other North African countries. It's so easy to make. This recipe, from the Catfish Institute, makes excellent use of the grain.

1/4 cup slivered almonds
2 Tbsp. olive oil
1 med. onion, chopped
2 cloves garlic, minced
2 med. carrots, cut on the diagonal
1 sm. red pepper, cored, seeded and cut into strips
1 tsp. ground coriander
2 cups chicken stock
4 Mississippi River catfish fillets cut into 2-inch strips
1 cup canned chickpeas, drained
1 med. zucchini, cut in half lengthwise, then into 1-inch strips
1 cup couscous or rice

Pan Size: Baking sheet *Oven Temp.: 350°* *Time: 8 minutes*

Toast almonds on a baking sheet. Heat oil in a large, heavy skillet and sauté onions, garlic, carrots, pepper and coriander. Add chicken broth and 2 cups water. Bring to a boil and cook for 5 minutes. Add catfish, chickpeas and zucchini and simmer for 15 minutes. Prepare couscous or rice according to package directions and place on a large serving plate, making a well in the center. Fill the well with the fish-vegetable mixture, reserving some of the broth and top with toasted almonds. Serve the cooking broth on the side.

EASY FISH CASSEROLE

4 servings

This stew-like casserole can be made with any available white fish fillet.

2 onions, sliced
2 lbs. red potatoes, sliced
1 tsp. butter
1 Tbsp. olive oil
2 Tbsp. minced garlic
3 Tbsp. fresh parsley
1 cup chicken broth
1 lb. fish fillets
2 cups frozen peas, thawed
2 cloves garlic, peeled and minced
2 Tbsp. oil
Salt and freshly-ground pepper, to taste

Pan Size: 3-qt. casserole *Oven Temp.: 350°* *Time: 45 minutes*

Spread the onion and potato slices along the bottom of greased casserole. Sprinkle with butter, oil, garlic, parsley, salt and ground pepper. Add broth and bake, covered, for 30 minutes or until potatoes are tender.

Arrange fish fillets on the potatoes. Add peas and garlic. Drizzle oil over the casserole and bake 15 minutes more. Uncover, season, and serve.

SHRIMP SCORPIO

3-4 servings

This is an excellent, easy dish. Serve it over fluffy white rice with a Greek salad. Add freshly baked Greek bread, a bottle of chilled, white Domestica wine (available in specialty shops) and you'll think you are dining in the Greek isles.

3 Tbsp. olive oil
2 onions, minced
2 tsp. minced garlic
1 Tbsp. finely minced dill
1/4 tsp. dry mustard
2 cups fresh or canned peeled tomatoes, chopped
1/2 cup tomato sauce
1/4 cup minced parsley
1 lb. lg. shrimp, peeled and deveined
1 cup crumbled feta cheese

Pan Size: 2-qt. casserole *Oven Temp.: 425°* *Time: 5 minutes*

Preheat oven. Heat oil in medium, 2-quart saucepan and add onions. Cook, stirring, until the onion starts to brown. Add garlic, parsley, dill, mustard, tomatoes and tomato sauce. Simmer, covered, for 30 minutes. Add shrimp to sauce and cook for 3 minutes or until shrimp turns pink. Pour the mixture into a buttered casserole and sprinkle with crumbled cheese. Bake until cheese starts to melt. Serve immediately.

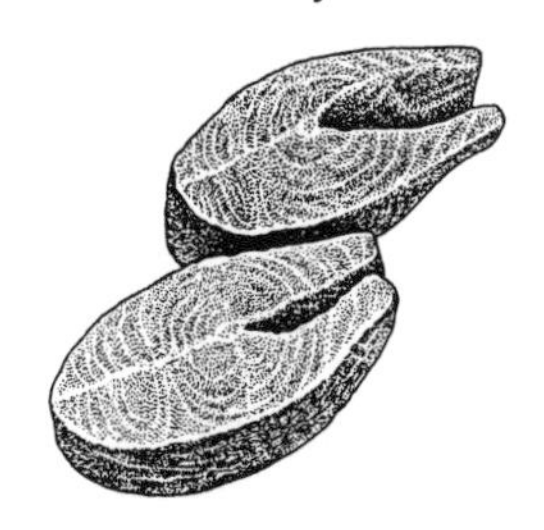

SAVORY SALMON STEAKS

2 servings

Put your microwave to work to make delicious and tender salmon steaks. Spray the baking dish with vegetable spray to prevent sticking. Serve the steaks with steamed rice and a green vegetable.

2 salmon steaks, cut 1-inch thick
1/4 cup low-fat plain yogurt
1 tsp. pepper
1 tsp. dill
2 tsp. minced fresh garlic

Pan Size: Microwavable dish *Temp.: HIGH* *Time: 8 minutes*

Place salmon steaks in a shallow microwavable dish. Top with yogurt, spices and garlic. Cover with vented plastic wrap. Microwave on HIGH for 8 minutes. Let stand 3 minutes before serving.
NOTE: This dish can also be cooked in a conventional oven. Preheat oven to 350°. Bake the salmon for 15 minutes or until it flakes easily with a fork.

SUPER SCALLOPS

2-3 servings

A quick and easy dish that's great with a side order of spaghetti cooked and tossed with butter and garlic and steamed broccoli.

2 tsp. butter or margarine
1 cup chopped scallions
2 cloves garlic, chopped
1 lb. sea scallops
1/2 cup chicken broth or white wine
1 Tbsp. fresh dill, chopped
Lemon wedges, for garnish

Heat butter in a frying pan. Add scallops, scallions and garlic. Sauté on medium heat for 5 minutes. Pour in broth or wine and simmer, uncovered, for 5 more minutes. Sprinkle dill over the scallops and serve with lemon wedges.

SHRIMP AND MUSSELS PAELLA

Makes 2-3 servings

Here's a great dish for any easy mid-week supper with little effort. It's also a hit with company!

1-1/2 cups instant brown rice
3 cups chicken broth
1 pkg. frozen mussels in hot sauce (I use Raimondi brand)
1 - 16 oz. pkg. instant frozen mixed vegetables
12 frozen shrimp
1 can mushrooms, drained
1 Tbsp. minced garlic
1 tsp. freshly-ground pepper

Pan Size: Microwave-proof dish Temp.: MEDIUM-HIGH Time: 20 minutes

Place rice and broth in a microwave-proof casserole or large pasta dish. Cover with vented plastic wrap. Cook on medium-high power for 5 minutes. Top with frozen mussels (remove from package). Cover loosely with plastic wrap and microwave for 10 minutes or until liquid is almost absorbed. Toss with the remaining ingredients and microwave 5 minutes more or until ingredients are steaming hot.

NOTE: Frozen fish are often fresher than so-called fresh fish you find in supermarkets. Check for package security.

SHRIMP CREOLE

Makes 3-4 servings

This is an invention – thanks in part to a Contadina recipe – that really tastes great and cooks up in no time! We love it so much we make it every week.

2 cups instant brown rice
2 cups water
1 Tbsp. soy sauce
1 cup frozen peas, not thawed
2 Tbsp. olive oil
1 cup chopped celery
1 cup chopped carrots
1 cup chopped onions
2 cloves garlic, chopped
1 cup chopped green or red pepper
1 - 14 oz. can chopped tomatoes
1 tsp. black pepper
1 tsp. garlic parsley
1 tsp. curry powder
1 lb. (about 20) frozen shrimp

Cook rice, water and soy sauce in a medium saucepan or Corning ware casserole over high heat until boiling; cover and reduce heat to simmer for 10 minutes or until liquid is absorbed. Stir in frozen peas and cover. Keep warm in a 300° oven.

In the meantime, in another large saucepan, heat the olive oil over medium high heat and add the vegetables, garlic and pepper. Sauté for 5 minutes, stirring often. Add the can of tomatoes and seasonings. Simmer for 10 minutes on low, covered. Add the shrimp and heat over medium heat for 2 to 3 minutes or until the shrimp are thawed and heated through. Serve over the heated rice.

ROASTED SHELL-ON SHRIMP

Makes 2-4 servings

I like this dish because it makes an easy appetizer for an easy meal that's perfect to share with friends. Add a nice bottle of white wine, a plate of Greek Country Salad, a crusty loaf of bread and you're all set to go!

1-1/2 lbs. lg. shrimp in the shell
3 Tbsp. extra-virgin olive oil
1 Tbsp. finely chopped parsley or dill
1/2 tsp. freshly grated lemon zest
2 cloves garlic, finely chopped
1/4 tsp.salt
Freshly ground pepper to taste

Preheat oven to 425°. Line a baking sheet with foil. Split shrimp along the back, using cooking shears to cut about two-thirds of the way, starting from head to tail.

Using the tip of a sharp knife, remove the black vein. Rinse shrimp thoroughly with cold water and pat dry. Place shrimp in a bowl and toss with remaining ingredients. Place cut side up on cookie sheets. Roast for 3 to 5 minutes or until shells turn pink. Serve.

CROCK POT RECIPES

A crock pot is a great investment! It's a time and energy saver that produces great meals in minimum effort.

GREEK CHICKEN STEW

Makes 4 servings

Put it on in the morning and come home to heaven! Serve with hot French bread and a salad.

- 4 sm. onions, peeled and quartered
- 4 carrots, scraped and cut into 1-inch slices
- 4 stalks celery, cut into 1-inch slices
- 2 sprigs fresh dill
- 4 sm. potatoes, peeled and quartered
- 1 lb. boneless chicken thighs
- 1 cup chicken broth
- 1/4 cup lemon juice
- 2 Tbsp. minced garlic
- 1 Tbsp. ground black pepper

Place all ingredients in a crock pot in the order given. Cover and cook on LOW for 8 hours. Or, cook on HIGH for 5 hours.

BEEF STEW

Makes 4 servings

Set this up in the morning and enjoy a hearty meal when you come home from work!

- 4 med. potatoes, peeled and cubed
- 4 carrots, scraped and cut into 1-inch pieces
- 4 stalks celery, cut into 1-inch pieces
- 2 onions, peeled and cut into quarters
- 4 cloves garlic, peeled and left whole
- 1 cup red wine
- 1 cup water
- 2 tsp. dried oregano
- 1 tsp. ground black pepper
- 2 tomatoes, chopped

Place all ingredients in the order given into the crock pot. Cover and cook on LOW for 6 to 8 hours. Serve with French bread.

MISCELLANEOUS

Garlic is the most versatile seasoning that lends itself to a wide array of foods – from all-purpose Garlic Butter to unusual Garlic Chip Cookies.

GARLIC BUTTER

Makes 3/4 cup

It pays to have ready-made garlic butter on hand to slather over fresh bread, toast, meats, vegetables or even pasta – anything that could use a dash of zippy flavor. It keeps for weeks in the refrigerator.

1/2 cup butter or margarine
3 cloves fresh garlic, finely minced

Mix butter by hand or with an electric mixer until creamy smooth. Add garlic and blend well. Store, covered, in the refrigerator or freezer for later use.

NOTE: You can increase the amount of garlic if you are a real aficionado. I use up to 6 cloves!

GARLIC MARINADE

Makes 1 cup

This aromatic marinade is superb on meat, fish, steaks, shellfish or poultry.

3/4 cup olive oil
3 cloves garlic, crushed
1/4 cup wine vinegar
1 tsp. oregano
Salt and freshly-ground pepper, to taste
1 tsp. Worcestershire sauce

Mix all ingredients well in a jar. Store in the refrigerator.

VARIATION #1: To add a real barbecue flavor for chicken or ribs, mix in 1/4 cup ketchup and 1/4 cup soy sauce.

VARIATION #2: For a sweeter marinade, ideal for chicken breasts, add 1/4 cup honey and 2 Tbsp. Dijon-style mustard.

SEASONING SALT

Makes 1/2 cup

Feel free to adapt this basic recipe to include your own favorite spices

2 Tbsp. garlic salt
2 Tbsp. white pepper
2 Tbsp. dried oregano
1/4 tsp. paprika
1/4 tsp. thyme
1/4 tsp. chili powder
1/4 tsp. curry powder

Blend well and store in a shaker-top jar, tightly covered, in a cool place.

TERIYAKI SAUCE

Makes 1 quart

You can make your own tasty, Oriental-style sauce at home. This keeps for months and is great on poultry, fish or game.

2 cups soy or Tamari sauce
1/4 cup honey
2 Tbsp. lemon juice
1/4 cup rice wine vinegar
1/4 cup dry sherry
1 2-inch piece fresh ginger
6 cloves garlic, peeled

Combine all ingredients in a blender, processing until smooth. Store in a glass jar in the refrigerator.

VEGETABLE RELISH

Makes 4 cups

This tasty recipe makes an ideal hostess gift.

4 med. carrots
2 med. onions
1 med. green pepper
1 cup chopped cabbage
1 cup green beans
1 cup wax beans
4 cloves garlic
2 cups sugar
2 cups cider or balsamic vinegar
2 Tbsp. celery seeds
2 Tbsp. mustard seeds

Cut up all vegetables. Place about 2 cups of them at a time in the blender. Cover with water. Add garlic. Process until coarsely chopped. Drain. Pour into a glass bowl or crock and cover with salted water.

Let stand at least 8 hours. Drain thoroughly, pressing out excess liquid. Mix vinegar, sugar, celery seed and mustard seed in a large saucepan. Heat to boiling. Stir in vegetables; reduce heat and simmer, uncovered, for 10 more minutes.

Pack into hot jars, leaving 1/4-inch head room. Seal well and process in boiling water for 10 minutes to sterilize.

GARLIC DILL PICKLES

Makes 6 quarts

There is nothing like the taste of homemade, garlic pickles! Do give these a try.

36 to 40 pickling cucumbers
(the smaller, the better)
7-1/2 cups water
5 cups white vinegar
1/2 cup pickling or non-iodized salt
12 cloves garlic, sliced
6 sprigs fresh dill
6 Tbsp. dill seed
6 slices onion

Wash and scrub cucumbers carefully, cutting a quarter-inch slice from the blossom end of each one. Heat water, vinegar and salt to the boiling point in a large Dutch oven. Place 2 cloves of garlic, 1 sprig of dill, 1 Tbsp. dill seed and 1 onion slice into each of 6 hot jars. Pack cucumbers neatly into the jars, allowing 1/2-inch head room. Cover with boiling brine. Seal and process in a boiling water bath to sterilize for 10 minutes.

SKORDALLA

Makes 3 cups

This traditional Greek recipe bases its unique flavor on the unusual combination of mashed potatoes and garlic. It can be served as an appetizer or as an ideal accompaniment to a festive dinner. It's one of my parents' favorite recipes and a recipe I am proud to pass on.

6 med. potatoes, peeled,
boiled and mashed
4 cloves garlic, crushed
1 cup olive oil
1/2 cup lemon juice or white
vinegar
3 egg yolks

Add hot mashed potatoes and garlic to the large bowl of an electric mixer. Beat well. Alternate slowly, adding the oil and lemon juice or vinegar. When the ingredients are thoroughly mixed, beat in the egg yolks to make the mixture fluffy. Chill before serving.

THE BEST PIZZA DOUGH

By making pizza at home, you get to add as much of your favorite toppings as you want! We usually make a large pizza, on a specially made pan with vent holes that allow for even cooking, and divide it in half – one side for my husband's meats and one side for my veggies.

But the real reason to make homemade pizza is so that you can add lots of garlic right into the crust!

1 cup warm water
1 pkg. rapid-rise yeast
1 tsp. sugar
1 tsp. salt
1/4 cup oil
2 Tbsp. garlic powder
1 Tbsp. oregano
3 cups flour, a mixture of all-purpose and whole wheat works well

Pan Size: Pizza pan *Oven Temp.: 500°* *Time: 20 minutes*

Dissolve yeast and sugar in warm water in a large bowl; let it stand until it starts to bubble. In the meantime, assemble the other ingredients.

Mix salt, oil, spices and 1 cup flour into the dissolved yeast. Beat well. Add remaining flour, 1/2 cup at a time, beating well with a wooden spoon. When you have a very stiff dough, use your hands to mix in just enough of the remaining flour so that your dough is no longer sticky. Knead 20 turns and place dough into a warm, oiled bowl. Cover with a damp towel or plastic wrap. Let it rise in a warm place for 30 minutes. Punch down the dough and pat onto a greased pizza pan. Let rise again for 20 minutes.

Top with your favorite, garlicky tomato sauce and choice of toppings. Place in a cold oven on the lowest rack, and turn the heat on. Bake until nicely browned.

Note: A pizza stone helps keep a crispy crust.

SPOT'S STEW

This recipe is from Andi Brown of Tampa, Florida. Andi makes enough food to feed her kitty, Spot, for about a month. You can use the same formula for dogs, too. Garlic helps keep fleas at bay.

2 onions, chopped
3/4 head of garlic – that's a whole head, not just a clove!
1 whole fryer chicken
1 lb. brown rice
1 cup broccoli, chopped
4 carrots
1 whole zucchini
1 whole yellow squash
1 handful green beans
2 stalks celery

In a 10-quart stainless steel stock pot, put 3 Tbsp. oil. Heat the oil and brown onions and garlic lightly. Add chicken and fill the pot with water. Simmer for 3 hours. Let cool and debone the chicken. Using an electric mixer, whip the ingredients into a purée. Put portions into ziplock bags and store in the freezer.

References

Chapter 1 — Things You Should Know About Garlic

1. Pinto, J.T. and Rivlin, R. S., "Antiproliferative Effects of Allium Derivatives of Garlic," *Journal of Nutrition*, Vol. 131, No. 3S, No 1058S.
2. Ibid.
3. Weil, Andrew, *Natural Health, Natural Medicine*. Boston, Houghton Mifflin, 1990, p. 238.
4. Kawashima, H. et al, "Clinical Experience with Kyoleopin (KLE). Clinical Study on General Fatigue Associated with Cold," published by the Medical College, Department of Third Medicine, Nihon University, Japan, 1985.
5. Nagai, K., "Experimental Studies on the Preventive Effect of Garlic Extract Against Infection with Influenza Virus," *Japanese Journal of Infectious Diseases*, Volume 47, 1973, p. 321.
6. Klosa, J., "Treatment of Colds with Garlic Oil," *Medical Monthly*, March 1950, p. 103.
7. Scheer, James F., "Garlic: Nature's Cure-all," *Bestways*, July 1981. p. 77.
8. Ibid., p. 78.
9. *Garlic Through the Ages*, undated report by Wakunaga of America.
10. Personal Communication.
11. Personal Communication.
12. Ushijima, M. et al, "Effect of Garlic and Garlic Preparations on Physiological and Psychological Stress in Mice," *Phytotherapeutic Research* Vol. 22: 226-44.
13. Ibid.
14. Kawashima, Hiroshi et al. "Anti-Fatigue Effect of Aged Garlic Extract in Athletic Club Students," *Preclinical and Clinical Reports,* 1986.
15. Polakovic, Gary, "Air Pollution Harmful to Babies, Fetuses, Studies Say," *Los Angeles Times,* December 17, 2001.
16. Lau, Benjamin, *Garlic Research Update.* Vancouver, B.C., Odyssey Publishing, 1991. P. 10.
17. Mindell, Earl, *Dr. Earl Mindell's Garlic – The Miracle Nutrient.* New Canaan, CT, Keats Publishing, Inc., 1994, p.113.
18. Lau, Benjamin, *Garlic and You*, Vancouver, B.C., Apple Publishing Company, 1997, p. 41.

19. Lau, Benjamin, *Garlic Research Update*. Vancouver, B.C., Odyssey Publishing, Inc., 1991, p. 19-20.
20. Jacobson, Michael F. et al. *Safe Food*, New York, Berkley Books, 1993, p. 60.
21. Hunter, Beatrice Trum, *The Mirage of Safety*. New York, Charles Scribner's Sons, 1975, p.13.
22. Ibid., p 24.
23. "Detoxification Using Aged Garlic," *The Health Professional*, Vol. 1, Number 1 (undated) p 2.

Chapter 2 — Dealing with Allergies, Arthritis, Alzheimer's and Aids

1. Langer, Stephen and Scheer, James F, *Pocket Guide to Natural Health*. New York, Kensington, 2001, p.6.
2. Personal Communication.
3. Kyo, E, et al, "Anti-Allergic Effects of Aged Garlic Extract," Phyomed 4(4): 335-340, 1997.
4. Ibid.
5. Carper, Jean, *Food: Your Miracle Medicine.* New York, HarperCollins Perennial, 1993, p. 384-385.
6. Ibid.
7. Personal Communication.
8. Johnson, R.J., "Aluminum: A Threat to Mental Health," *Bestways.* December, 1985, pp. 28-29.
9. Casdorph, Richard and Walker, Morton, *Toxic Metal Syndrome*. Garden City Park, New York, Avery Publishing Group, 1995, pp. 115-116.
10. Murray, Frank, *The Big Family Guide to All Minerals.* New Canaan, CT, Keats Publishing, 1995, p.376.
11. Lemonick, Michael D. and Park, Alice, "The Nun Study," *Time,* May 14, 2001.
12. Gwebu, E. et al, "Protection of NGH-Differentiated PC12 Cells by Aged Garlic Extract from the Cytotoxicity of Beta Amyloid," Society for Neuroscience, Volume 24, 1998.
13. Abdullah, Tariq, et al, "Garlic Revisited: Therapeutic for the Major Diseases of Our Times*?" Journal of the National Medical Association,* Vol. 50, No. 4, 1988.
14. Lau, Benjamin, Garlic and You: *The Modern Medicine*, Vancouver, British Columbia, Apple Publishing, 1997, p. 9.
15. Ibid., p. 68.
16. Ibid., p. 102.
17. Chaudbury, D.S., et al, "Therapeutic Usefulness of Garlic in Leprosy," *Journal of the Indian Medical Association*:39-517, 1962.

Chapter 3 — New Weapon Against TB, Sickle Cell Anemia and Ulcers

1. Martin, Simon, "Superbugs: Is This The Final Warning?" from his book *Candida.* London, Element, 1998.
2. Rodale, J.I., *The Complete Book of Food and Nutrition.* Emmaus, PA. Rodale Books, Inc., 1961, pp.493-495.
3. *Prevention Natural Healing Guide 2000*, Prevention, Emmaus, PA, Rodale, Inc., 2000, p.85.
4. Duke, James A., *The Green Pharmacy*, Emmaus. PA, Rodale Press, 1997, p. 433.
5. "Excerpts from Recent Advances on the Nutritional Benefits Accompanying the Use of Garlic as a Supplement," Newport Beach, California Garlic Conference, November 15-17, 1998, p. 3.
6. Ibid.
7. Ibid.
8. Ibid., p. 4.
9. "Support for Sickle Cell Anemia," *Research Update on Aged Garlic Extract,* Wakunaga of America, Vol. 13, 2001.
10. Personal communication, 2001.
11. Sivam, G. P., "Protection Against Helicobacter pylori and Other Bacterial Infections by Garlic," *Journal Nutrition* 131: 1106S-1108S, 2001.
12. Ibid.
13. Ibid.

Chapter 4 — Supplemental Insurance for Heart and Arteries

1. Adams, Ruth and Murray, Frank, *All You Should Know About Health Foods,* New York, Larchmont Books, 1975, pp. 102-103.
2. Lau, Benjamin. *Garlic and You.* Vancouver, B.C., Apple Publishing Company, Ltd., 1997, p. 13.
3. Ibid.
4. Chang, M. I., Johnson, M. A., "Effect of Garlic on Carbohydrate Metabolism and Lipid Synthesis in Rats," *Journal Nutrition* 110:931, 1980.
5. Lau, Benjamin, *Garlic and You*, Vancouver, B.C., Apple Publishing Company, 1997, p 13-14.
6. Adenumbi, M. A., and Lau, B.H.S., "Inhibition of in Vitro Germination and Spherulation of Coccidioides Immitus by Allium Sativum," *Current Microbial* 13:73, 1986.
7. Lau, Benjamin, *Garlic and You.* Vancouver, B.C., Apple Publishing Company, 1997, p. 14.
8. Ibid., p. 14-15.
9. Ibid., p. 14-15.

10. Ide, N. and Lau, B.H.S., "Garlic Compounds Inhibit Low Density Lipoprotein (LDL) Oxidation and Protect Endothelial Cells from Oxidized LDL-Induced Injury," FASEB Journal 11(3):A 122 #713.
11. Geng, Z and Lau, B.H.S., "Aged Garlic Extract Modulates Glutathione Redox Cycle and Superoxide dismutase Activity in Vascular Endothelial Cells," *Phytotherapy Research* 11:54-56 and Efendy, J.L. et al, "The Effect of Aged Garlic Extract, 'Kyolic' on the development of Experimental Atheroclerosis," *Atherosclerosis* 132: 37-42.
12. Langer, Stephen and Scheer, James F., *Solved: The Riddle of Illness,* Los Angeles, Keats Publishing, Inc., 2000, p.126.
13. Ibid.
14. Rath, Matthias, "How Vitamin C Prevents Heart Attack and Stroke," a publication of the Linus Pauling Heart Foundation, 1992.
15. D'Angelo, A. and Selhub, J. "Homocysteine and Thrombotic Disease," *Blood,* 90: 1-11 In Pietrzik, K and Bronstrup, A., *Annals of Nutrition Metabolism* 41: 331-343.
16. Naruszewicz, M. et al, "Thiolation of Low Density Lipoprotein by Homocysteine," *Nutrition Metabolism Cardiovascular Discovery*: 4: 70-77, 1994.
17. Yeh, Y., et al, "Garlic Extract Reduces Plasma Concentration of Homocysteine in Rate Rendered Folic Acid Deficiency,: FASEB 13: (4): A232; #209.12
18. Press Release, Gordon Research, January 30, 2001.
19. Murray, Michael and Pizzorno, Joseph, *Encyclopedia of Natural Medicine.* Rocklin, CA, Prima Publishing, 1998, p. 100.
20. "Garlic . . . Just a Gimmick?" Associated Press story, October 2, 1992.
21. Privatera, James R. and Stang, Alan, *Silent Clots – Life's Biggest Killer.* Covina, California. The Catacombs Press, 1996, pp. 2-3.
22. Bolton, S et al, "The Medical Uses of Garlic – Fact or Fiction," *American Pharmacy* 22:448, 1985.
23. Lau, Benjamin, *Garlic and You.* Vancouver, B.C., Apple Publishing Co., Ltd., 1997, p.27.
24. Ibid.
25. Agel, M. B. et al, "Direct Relaxant Effects of Garlic Juice on Smooth and Cardiac Muscles," Journal Ethnopharmacology 33:13, 1991.
26. Das, I et al, "Nitric Oxide Synthase Activation is a Unique Mechanism of Garlic Action," *Biochemical Society Transactions*, 23: 136S, 1995.
27. Fackelmann, K.A., "Stress Puts Squeeze on Clogged Vessels," *Science News,* November 16, 1991, p. 309.
28. Justice, Blair, *Who Gets Sick*, Houston, Peak Press, 1987, p. 55.

Chapter 5 — Promising Answer to Cancer, Aging and Memory Loss

1. Wigley, C., "Chemical Carcinogenesis and Precancer," in the *Introduction to the Cellular and Molecular Biology of Cancer*, Franks, L.M. and Teich, N., editors, 1986, p. 131.
2. Ames, Bruce, N., et al, "Oxidants, Anti-Oxidants and Degenerative Diseases in Aging," *Proceedings of the National Academy of Science,* Vol.90, Sept., 1993; 7915-7922.
3. Pinto, John F. and Rivlin, Richard S., "Garlic and Allium Vegetables in Cancer Prevention," *Nutritional Oncology,* 1999. P. 393.
4. Ibid., p. 401.
5. I-Sin Lin, Robert, *Garlic and Health*, Irvine, California, International Academy of Health Fitness, 1994, p. 21.
6. Lau, Benjamin, *Garlic and You*. Vancouver, B.C., Apple Publishing, 1997, p. 50.
7. Lin, Robert I, "Garlic Power," a publication of the International Academy of Health & Fitness, Irvine, CA, April 30, 1990.
8. Ibid.
9. Personal Communication.
10. I. San Lin, Robert, *Garlic and Health*, Irvine, CA, International Academy of Health and Fitness, 1994, pp. 17-18.
11. Ibid.
12. Clarke, Mary, "Eating Fat, Then and Now." Special Report, Kansas State University, 1996.
13. I. San-Lin, Robert, *Garlic and Health*. Irvine, CA., International Academy of Health and Fitness, 1994, pp. 17-18.
14. Murray, Michael and Pizzorno, Joseph, *Encyclopedia of Natural Medicine*. Rocklin, CA, Prima Publishing, 1998, pp. 49-51.
15. Weiner, Michael and Weiner, Janet A., *Herbs That Heal*. Mill Valley, CA, Quantum Books, 1994, p. 160.
16. Ibid.
17. "Nutrition Garlic Compounds Indicated to Inhibit Mammary Tumor Formation," *Cancer Weekly Plus,* March 24, 1997.
18. Fleischauer, A.T. and Arab, Lenore, "Garlic and Cancer; A Critical Review of the Epidemiologic Literature," *The Journal of Nutrition*, Vol. 131, No. 3S, March 2001, 1032S-1040S.
19. Lau, Benjamin S., *Garlic And You*. Vancouver, B.C., Apple Publishing Company Limited, 1997, p. 46.
20. Mindell, Earl, *Dr. Earl Mindell's Garlic: The Miracle Nutrient*. New Canaan, CT. Keats Publishing, Inc., 1994, p. 86.
21. Steinmetz, K.A, et al, "Vegetables, Fruits and Lung Cancer in the Iowa Women's Health Study," *Cancer Research* 53:536, 1993.
22. Lau, Benjamin, *Garlic and You*. Vancouver, B.C., Apple Publishing Company Limited, 1997, p. 46.
23. Pinto, J.Y. and Rivlin, R.S., "Garlic and Prevention of Prostate Cancer," Chapter

18 in Neutraceuticals: *Designer Foods: Garlic, Soy and Licorice,* Lanchance, P. P. (ed.) Trumbell, CT. Food & Nutrition Press, pp. 177-187.
24. Lau, Benjamin, *Garlic Research Update*, Vancouver, B.C., Odyssey Publishing, Inc., 1991, p. 15.
25. Ibid., p. 16.
26. Ibid., p. 21.
27. Lamm, D.L. and Riggs, D.R., "Enhanced Immunocompetence by Garlic Role in Bladder Cancer and Other Malignancies," *The Journal of Nutrition*, March, 2001, Vol. 131, No. 35, p. 1067S.
28. Ibid.
29. Ibid.
30. Ibid., p. 90.
31. Lau, Benjamin, *Garlic and You.* Vancouver, B.C., Apple Publishing Company, 1997, p. 47.
32. Leonov, Sergiev and I., "Use of Garlic Paste on Pre-Cancerous Lips," *Problems of Oncology*, March/April, 1958.
33. Ibid., p. 51.
34. Gaynor, Mitchell L. and Hickey, Jerry, *Dr. Gaynor's Cancer Prevention Program.* New York, Kensington Books, p 211, 1999.
35. Block, Eric, *Scientific American*, Volume 252, pp. 114-118, 1985.
36. Zhang, Y.X., "Ameliorating Effect of Aged Garlic Extract (AGE) on Learning Behaviors in Thymectomized Senescence Accelerated Mouse, in *Senescence Accelerated Mouse*, T. Takada editor, Elsevier Science B.V., pp. 447-450.
37. Personal Communication.
38. Muscular Development, September, 2001, p. 42.

Chapter 6 — Super Natural Antibiotic

1. Lau, Benjamin, *Garlic and You*. Vancouver, B.C., Apple Publishing, 1997, pp. 3-4.
2. Lau, Benjamin, *Garlic Research Update*. Vancouver, B.C., Odyssey Publishing, Inc., 1991, p. 4.
3. Ibid., pp. 5-6.
4. Mindell, Earl, *Dr. Earl Mindell's Garlic, The Miracle Nutrient.* New Canaan, CT., Keats Publishing, Inc., 1994, p. 95.
5. Ibid., p. 96.
6. Ibid., p. 98 and *The New Columbia Encyclopedia*. New York City, Columbia University Press, 1975, p. 2451.
7. Lau, Benjamin, *Garlic Research Update,* Vancouver, B.C., Odyssey Publishing, Inc., 1994, p. 6.
8. Ibid.
9. Lau, Benjamin. *Garlic and You*. Vancouver, B.C., Apple Publishing., 1997, p. 9.

Chapter 7 — Multi-Purpose Health Booster

1. Weiner, Michael A. and Weiner, Janet A., *Herbs That Heal,* Mill Valley, CA, Quantum Books, 1994, pp. 160-161.

Chapter 9 — Aged Garlic – The Inside Story

1. Amagase, H. et al, "Intake of Garlic and its Bioactive Components," presented at the conference, "Recent Advances on the Nutritional Benefits Accompanying the Use of Garlic as a Supplement," Newport Beach, CA, November 15-17, 1998.
2. Mindell, Dr. Earl, *Dr. Earl Mindell's Garlic, The Miracle Nutrient.* New Canaan, CT., Keats Publishing, Inc., 1994, p. 20.
3. Walker, Morton, "Garlic," *Heath Foods Business*, May, 1994, p. 50.
4. Mindell, Earl, *Dr. Earl Mindell's Garlic: The Miracle Nutrient.* New Canaan, CT., Keats Publishing, Inc., 1994, p. 18.
5. Papp, Leslie, "An Investigation into Alternative Medicine," *Toronto Star,* January 15, 2000.
6. Musgrave, Nan, "Garlic's Sweet Smell of Success," *ITA Journal*, March, 1991.
7. Amagase, Harunobu et al, "Intake of Garlic and its Bioactive Components," presented at the Conference "Recent Advances on the Nutritional Benefits Accompanying the Use of Garlic as a Supplement," November 15-17, 1998 in Newport Beach, CA.
8. "Unusually Low Incidence of Death from Myocardial Infarction (heart attack)," *The Journal of the American Medical Association*, 188:845, June 8, 1964.

ABOUT JAMES F. SCHEER

Some years ago the late Irving Wallace, writer of *The Prize*, *The Man*, and *The Chapman Report,* among many other best-selling novels, heard Jim Scheer give a talk and came up to him and said, "You express yourself so well that you ought to write for a living."

Jim decided to give it a try and enrolled in the University of Wisconsin's School of Journalism. Since he graduated, the appearance of more than 2,000 of his articles and columns in more than 105 magazines worldwide are making him think that Irving Wallace may have been right.

Aside from writing for *Redbook*, *Good Housekeeping*, *Cosmopolitan, Better Homes & Gardens* and a half dozen health/nutrition magazines, he has served as editor of three nutrition/health magazines, including *Let's Live*, now topping 1.7 million in circulation. Twenty-two of his books – mainly in nutrition and health – have been published by McGraw-Hill, Doubleday, Pocket Books and others.

Solved: The Riddle of Illness (with Stephen Langer, MD, of Berkeley, CA), now in its Third Edition, has sold more than 100,000 copies and was characterized by Dr. Wayne Dyer as "one of the most important books of our time." In its first edition, *Solved: The Riddle of Illness* was a selection of the Prevention Book Club and on the Ingram best-seller list for 12 weeks. It was chosen by a panel of authorities to be condensed in the book, *The Best of Health*, among the top quality health books ever written. The late Nobel Laureate Dr. Linus Pauling headed that panel.

Another of his best-sellers, *Foods That Heal* (with Maureen Salaman), sold more than a million copies at $19.95. His latest books are *The Magic of Chia* (Revival of an Ancient Wonder Food) and the *Pocket Guide to Natural Health,* the latter with Dr. Langer.

One of his seven books in areas other than nutrition/health served as the basis for Hollywood producer David Wolper's 60-minute documentary, *The Race for Space*, which was nominated for an Academy Award and, later, voted the winner in its category at the San Francisco International Film Festival.

ABOUT LYNN ALLISON

A divorce changed Montreal-born Lynn Allison from a woman who had everything to a woman who had nothing – well, except two young daughters to support and no employment.

Necessity transformed her into a woman who could do something about her situation. Loving to write, she created self-help articles for local newspapers that brought enthusiastic response, encouraging her to apply for and win positions hosting local cable TV interview shows. Her charisma and ability to ask questions that drew out revealing answers from guests led to the Canadian Broadcasting System offering her the hostess position on a national TV talk show.

Concurrently, she was writing alternative health and nutrition articles for *Globe Communications.* An offer for her to join Vision Cable in Tampa, Florida induced her to move to the USA. Her boss at *Globe Communications* followed her to Tampa, where they married in 1986. When *Globe,* the tabloid she had worked for in Montreal, hired her for full-time writing at its headquarters in Boca Raton, she and her husband moved there.

Several years later, Lynn decided to write at home to be with her children and what she calls her zoo – dogs and cats. A prolific writer, Lynn still contributes to the *Globe,* and has written weekly food column for area newspapers. More than 30 of her books have been published, among them *Natural Stress Busters for the Whole Family, the Doctor's Quick Weight Loss Diet, Low Impact Aerobics, Brand Name Fast Food Calorie Counter, Spice Up Your Holiday Meals,* and others.

Lynn edits her own bimonthly health and fitness newsletter, acts as medical consultant to several Florida media outlets and is a certified aerobics instructor, holding a certificate in Sports Nutrition. She advocates an "everything in moderation" philosophy of life, as well as a down-to-earth, common sense approach to coping with everyday issues. Her hobbies include reading, practicing yoga, playing with Marty, her black Labrador, and the rest of her zoo and creating "to die for" garlic-laced recipes, many of which appear in this book.

ABOUT CHARLIE FOX

To many people garlic is just garlic, a flavoring that gives zest to food. To Charlie Fox, it is the difference between life and death. More than 33 years ago, while Charlie was working in his father's floor wax business, breathing toxic fumes daily – particularly carbon tetrachloride, one of the most potent cancer causatives — he became deathly ill.

Doctors found that three-fourths of his liver was damaged. and said that his chances of continuing to live were marginal. Charlie didn't like the odds, so he made drastic life changes. A raw food diet, daily exercise, pure water and an abundance of garlic rejuvenated his liver and the rest of him. Today he is noted for super-energy and stamina. He attributes this mainly to garlic.

Fascinated with garlic's effectiveness against illnesses from times of the ancient Chinese, Greeks and Romans until now, Charlie noted that hundreds of modern studies validate its health value. Twenty-two years ago, this motivated him to join Wakunaga of America, makers of aged garlic, and to study intensively the many benefits of garlic. Inasmuch as Charlie has given thousands of talks on this subject – in person and on the air — throughout the United States, Canada, Australia, New Zealand, Malaysia, Singapore and Japan, he has come to be known as "The Garlic Guru."

"Prevention is the best medicine, and the greatest doctor in the world is the physician inside – Dr. Immune," he tells listeners. For many decades, audiences have asked him, "When are you going to write a book on garlic?"

This is it, written with a little help from his friends – Lynn Allison and Jim Scheer.

INDEX

To order additional copies of
THE GARLIC CURE
please complete the following.

$14.95 EACH
(plus $3.95 shipping & handling for first book,
add $2.00 for each additional book ordered.

Shipping and Handling costs for larger quantites
available upon request.

Please send me ______ additional books at $14.95 + shipping & handling

Bill my: ❏ VISA ❏ MasterCard Expires __________

Card # ______________________________

Signature ______________________________

Daytime Phone Number ______________________________

For credit card orders call 1-888-568-6329
TO ORDER ON-LINE VISIT: www.jmcompanies.com
OR SEND THIS ORDER FORM TO:
Alpha Omega Press
PO Box 248, 407 Hwy 13 East
Gwinner, ND 58040

I am enclosing $____________ ❏ Check ❏ Money Order
Payable in US funds. No cash accepted.

SHIP TO:

Name ______________________________

Mailing Address ______________________________

City ______________________________

State/Zip ______________________________

Orders by check allow longer delivery time.
Money order and credit card orders will be shipped within 48 hours.
This offer is subject to change without notice.

ALPHA OMEGA PRESS

a division of

Alpha Omega, Inc.
3303 Fiechtner Drive SW, Suite 100
Fargo, ND 58103
800-972-3114